5–10-Minute
BIBLE STORIES
for Modern Teens

Aria Wrenley

Aria Wrenley© Copyright 2025
All rights reserved.

Protected with www.protectmywork.com

This document is geared towards providing exact and reliable information in regard to the topic and issue covered.

In no way is it legal to reproduce, duplicate, or transmit any part of this document in either electronic means or in printed format. All rights reserved.

The information provided herein is stated to be truthful and consistent, in that any liability, in terms of inattention or otherwise, by any usage or abuse of any policies, processes, or directions contained within is the solitary and utter responsibility of the recipient reader. Under no circumstances will any legal responsibility or blame be held against the publisher for any reparation, damages, or monetary loss due to the information herein, either directly or indirectly.

Respective authors own all copyrights not held by the publisher.

The information herein is offered for informational purposes solely and is universal as so. The presentation of the information is without a contract or any type of guarantee assurance.

The trademarks that are used are without any consent, and the publication of the trademark is without permission or backing by the trademark owner. All trademarks and brands within this book are for clarifying purposes only and are owned by the owners themselves, not affiliated with this document.

Contents

Introduction 1

    A Note to Parents & Educators 2

    Dear Reader One Story a Day or One Story a Week 4

    Reading Plans — 50 Days and 50 Weeks Checklists 8

Part I Beginnings (Genesis) 9

1. Light, Life, and Purpose — Creation
   (Genesis 1–2) 10

2. When Trust Broke — The Fall
   (Genesis 3) 13

3. Jealousy at the Door — Cain & Abel
   (Genesis 4) 16

4. Build What's Good — Noah & the Ark
   (Genesis 6–9) 19

5. One Language, Many Plans — Tower of Babel
   (Genesis 11:1–9) 22

Part II Promise & Family (Genesis 12–50) 25

6. Go—Even Without a Map — Call of Abram
   (Genesis 12:1–9) 26

7. A Promise with a Sign — Covenant with Abraham
   (Genesis 15; 17) 29

8. Seen in the Wilderness — Hagar & Ishmael
   (Genesis 16; 21:8–21) 32

9. Laughter Arrives — Birth of Isaac
   (Genesis 21:1–7) 35

10. When Love Is Tested — Abraham & Isaac
    (Genesis 22) 38

11. A Ladder in the Dark — Jacob's Dream
    (Genesis 28:10–22) 41

12	When Family Hurts — Joseph's Dreams & Betrayal (Genesis 37)	44
13	From Pit to Purpose — Joseph in Egypt (Genesis 39–41)	47
14	Grace Wins — Joseph Forgives (Genesis 45; 50:15–21)	50

Part III Rescue & A New Way to Live (Exodus–Joshua)   53

15	Protected on the River — Moses in the Basket (Exodus 2:1–10)	54
16	A Voice from Fire — Burning Bush (Exodus 3)	57
17	A Night of Freedom — Plagues & Passover (Exodus 7–12)	60
18	Walk Through the Impossible — Red Sea (Exodus 14)	63
19	Stone Words, Living Way — Ten Commandments (Exodus 19–20)	66
20	Daily Bread — Manna in the Wilderness (Exodus 16)	69
21	Walls That Fall — Joshua & Jericho (Joshua 6)	72

Part IV Courage & Kindness (Judges–Ruth–1 Samuel)   75

22	Lead Like Deborah — Deborah the Judge (Judges 4–5)	76
23	Less Is More — Gideon's 300 (Judges 6–7)	79
24	Loyalty that Shines — Ruth & Boaz (Ruth)	82
25	From Tears to Calling — Hannah & Samuel (1 Samuel 1–3)	85

Part V Heart after God (1-2 Samuel, 1 Kings) — 89

26 Facing Giants — David & Goliath (1 Samuel 17) 90

27 Mercy When You Can Win — David Spares Saul (1 Samuel 24) 93

28 Dance Like No One's Watching — David's Heart for God (2 Samuel 6) 96

29 Ask for Wisdom — Solomon's Prayer (1 Kings 3) 99

Part VI Fire & Whispers (1-2 Kings) — 103

30 Fire on the Mountain — Elijah vs. Prophets of Baal (1 Kings 18) 104

31 A Quiet Voice Still Speaks — Elijah at Horeb (1 Kings 19:1-18) 107

32 A Small Jar, Big Hope — Elisha & the Widow's Oil (2 Kings 4:1-7) 110

33 When You're Afraid — Hezekiah's Prayer (2 Kings 20; Isaiah 38) 113

Part VII Stand Firm (Esther, Jonah, Daniel, Nehemiah) — 117

34 A Second Chance — Jonah & the Big Fish (Jonah) 118

35 For Such a Time — Esther Saves Her People (Esther) 121

36 Lions Lose Tonight — Daniel in the Lions' Den (Daniel 6) 124

37 Rebuild What's Broken — Nehemiah & the Wall (Nehemiah 1-6) 127

Part VIII God With Us (Gospels: Birth & Early Days) — 131

- **38** Hope in a Manger — Birth of Jesus (Luke 2; Matthew 1-2) 132
- **39** About My Father's Business — Boy Jesus in the Temple (Luke 2:41-52) 135
- **40** Ready for the Mission — Baptism & Temptation (Matthew 3-4) 138

Part IX Teachings & Miracles (Gospels: Ministry) — 141

- **41** Follow Me — Calling the Disciples (Matthew 4:18-22; Luke 5) 142
- **42** The Upside-Down Way — Beatitudes (Matthew 5:1-12) 145
- **43** Peace in the Storm — Jesus Calms the Sea (Mark 4:35-41) 148
- **44** More Than Enough — Feeding the 5,000 (John 6:1-14) 151
- **45** Neighbor Means Everyone — Good Samaritan (Luke 10:25-37) 154
- **46** You Can Always Come Home — Prodigal Son (Luke 15:11-32) 157
- **47** Seen in the Crowd — Zacchaeus (Luke 19:1-10) 160

Part X Cross, Empty Tomb & New Start (Gospels-Acts) — 163

- **48** Served at the Table — Last Supper & Gethsemane (Luke 22; John 13) 164
- **49** Love Wins — Cross & Resurrection (Luke 23-24; John 20) 167
- **50** Power to Begin — Pentecost & the Early Church (Acts 2; 4:32-35) 170

Introduction

A Note to Parents & Educators

Thank you for choosing to walk alongside a teen's faith journey. This book was created to help young readers between 13 and 16 connect with timeless truths in a way that feels alive, real, and personal. The goal is simple: to make the Bible approachable and meaningful, not distant or difficult. Every page was written with the heart of a mentor and the curiosity of a teen in mind—bridging generations while keeping faith practical and inspiring.

You can use this book in many ways. At home, it can become a quiet daily reflection, a conversation starter around the table, or part of a bedtime routine that replaces a few minutes of scrolling with something uplifting. In youth groups or classrooms, it can guide weekly discussions, encourage journaling, or open honest dialogue about life's challenges. The stories were chosen and retold to spark thought, not to preach—to show how faith can be lived, questioned, and grown with courage and authenticity.

Each chapter follows the same rhythm to make reading simple and familiar. It begins with a short story drawn from Scripture, told in language that brings the ancient world close to today's experience. After the story, a section called What It Means helps explain the heart of the message in easy, natural terms. Life Lesson turns that message into something usable—a principle that speaks to friendship, purpose, confidence, or forgiveness. Try This invites the reader to take a small, real-world step during the week, putting faith into action through kindness, service, or reflection. There's also a short Did You Know? box with a cultural or historical fact to deepen understanding, and a few Words to Know that clarify key terms. Finally, a simple Short Prayer closes each reading, followed by Read More—a direct link to the Scripture passage itself, for those who wish to go deeper.

Feel free to adapt the pace. Some teens may read one story a day as a five-minute devotional; others may prefer one per week, taking time to discuss or journal about it. There is no single right way to move through these pages. What matters most is consistency—the quiet habit of returning again and again to listen, learn, and grow.

If you are a parent, this book is a doorway to meaningful conversations. Teens may not always say much, but stories have a way of unlocking what's hidden. Read together occasionally, ask what part stood out, and listen more than you speak. If you are an educator, mentor, or youth leader, think of this book as a flexible tool. You can read the stories aloud, use the Try This challenges for group projects, or let students share their reflections in their own words.

Above all, remember that this isn't about finishing a checklist—it's about forming a connection. The Bible is full of people who doubted, failed, tried again, and discovered grace along the way. That same journey is open to every teen who picks up this book. Your support, encouragement, and presence make all the difference. May these pages become a shared space of curiosity, honesty, and hope—one story at a time.

Dear Reader One Story a Day or One Story a Week

Hey there. Before you dive in, take a breath. This isn't another school book or a list of things you have to memorize. It's a journey made of fifty short stories that carry the heartbeat of something ancient and alive. Some of these stories you might already know a little about—others might surprise you. But all of them are here to show that faith isn't something you only think about in church; it's something that can grow quietly in your everyday life, even when things feel messy, confusing, or ordinary.

You don't need to rush. Each story was written to take just a few minutes—long enough to think, short enough to fit into your day. You can read one every morning before school, or one every night before you sleep. If you prefer, stretch it out and read one story each week, letting it stay with you as the days unfold. What matters most isn't speed—it's what happens inside you while you read.

As you move through these pages, you'll find a rhythm that repeats. Every story begins with a real moment from Scripture, told in a way that helps you picture it, feel it, and understand what the people in it were facing. Then you'll see how it connects to life now—to your own questions about purpose, friendship, pressure, or hope. There's a short challenge you can try, something simple that turns belief into action. You'll also find fun facts that help you see the world of the Bible as real and human, and a few words explained so nothing feels confusing. Each story ends with a short prayer—not because you have to pray it perfectly, but because it's a quiet way to say, "I'm here, and I'm listening."

Introduction

This book isn't about rules or perfection. It's about curiosity—about noticing that faith isn't something distant or impossible, but something that keeps showing up in real life, even in the smallest ways. If you miss a day, no problem. Just come back. If you don't understand something, that's okay too. Keep reading, keep wondering, keep asking questions. That's how real faith grows.

Maybe you'll read this on your own, maybe with a parent, a friend, or a group. However you choose, make it yours. Bring your thoughts, your doubts, your laughter, your what-ifs. Let every story meet you where you are, and don't worry about where you should be. You're already on the journey.

So grab a quiet moment, open to the first story, and see what happens. One story a day. Or one story a week. Either way, each one can plant a seed—and over time, those seeds can grow into something strong and steady: a faith that feels like your own.

Thank you for reading!

You'll find our note

of gratitude on page 115

Aria Wrenley

Story Flow

Every story in this book follows a simple rhythm meant to guide you—not to lecture, but to lead you through something real. Think of it like a conversation that unfolds step by step. It begins with the story itself, told in a way that helps you imagine it happening right in front of you. You'll meet people who faced impossible odds, made tough choices, or found courage they didn't know they had. These aren't fairy tales. They're moments from the Bible retold so you can see how faith looked when it was tested, alive, and human.

After the story, you'll find a short section called What It Means. This is where we pause to uncover what's at the heart of the story—why it mattered back then and why it still matters now. It's not about memorizing lessons or rules; it's about discovering truth that connects across time. You'll see how these ancient moments can mirror your own life—how the struggles, friendships, hopes, and fears of people thousands of years ago aren't all that different from what you face today.

Then comes Life Lesson. This is where things turn practical. Each lesson takes the meaning of the story and shows you how it plays out in everyday life—in how you treat others, how you handle pressure, or how you find purpose when things feel uncertain. These lessons are short, but they're meant to stick with you, like a quiet reminder you carry through the week.

The next part, Try This, makes it real. Here, you'll find a small challenge or action you can actually do—something simple but meaningful that brings the story off the page and into your world. It might be an act of kindness, a habit of gratitude, or a moment of reflection that helps you see faith in motion. None of these challenges are about being perfect. They're about practice—small steps that shape who you're becoming.

You'll also come across Did You Know?—a quick fact about history, geography, or culture that gives you a glimpse of what life was like when these stories happened. Maybe you'll learn what an ancient city really looked like, or what certain traditions meant. These little details make the Bible world feel less distant, helping you picture the places and people more clearly.

To make sure nothing feels confusing, each story includes Words to Know. These are short explanations of terms that might be new or unfamiliar—things like "covenant," "prophet," or "mercy." They're there to make reading easier, not harder, so you can focus on what the story is really saying.

At the end, you'll find a Short Prayer. It's not long or formal—just a few honest words to help you pause and talk with God in your own way. You can read it out loud, whisper it, or simply think it quietly. It's a way to end each reading with peace, gratitude, and focus.

Finally, there's Read More, where you'll see the exact Bible passages the story came from. You can open your own Bible and read them for yourself if you want to go deeper. That's where these stories began, and going back to them can make everything come alive in a new way.

That's the flow—simple, clear, and built to grow with you. The goal isn't to finish the book quickly or to know every answer. It's to slow down, listen, and let each story work its way into your heart. Over time, you'll notice something changing: the stories won't just teach you about faith—they'll help you live it.

Reading Plans — 50 Days and 50 Weeks Checklists

Every journey begins with a rhythm. The stories in this book are designed to fit your life—whether you like moving fast or taking things slow. That's why there are two reading paths: a 50-day plan and a 50-week plan. Both lead to the same destination, but the pace is yours to choose.

If you want a daily habit, the 50-day plan is the perfect start—fifty short readings, one each day, just a few minutes to pause, reflect, and reconnect. These quiet moments often become something more—a steady source of calm, focus, and strength in the middle of busy days.

If you'd rather take your time, the 50-week plan lets each story sink in over a week. It's great for youth groups, Sunday classes, or family reading nights. Read once, think about it during your week, and let its message grow naturally.

Neither plan is about pressure or perfection. You can miss a day, change your pace, or mix both paths as life changes. What matters most is showing up—because faith grows in small, steady moments.

The checklists at the end of this section will help you track your progress, reminding you that every story read is another step forward. There's no finish line here—only a journey toward peace, courage, and purpose, one story at a time.

Part I
Beginnings
(Genesis)

Light, Life, and Purpose — Creation (Genesis 1-2)

Before there was sound, color, or shape, there was only silence. Darkness stretched without end—no stars, no wind, no time. And then, a voice spoke: "Let there be light."

The silence shattered as brilliance poured across the emptiness. Shadows fled, and warmth filled what had never been warm. Light met darkness, day met night, and the rhythm of life began. The voice spoke again, separating the oceans from the sky, shaping land from water. Mountains rose, rivers ran, and soft rain kissed the earth awake.

Green spread everywhere—grass, vines, trees heavy with fruit. The world began to hum with movement and color.

The sun took its place to mark the day, the moon and stars to watch over the night. The world glowed with newness.

Then the seas stirred with life. Fish darted beneath the waves, and birds burst into the sky, their wings flashing against the sunlight. Every living thing had a purpose, each different yet connected. The Creator saw it all and smiled—it was good.

But something was missing. Creation was alive, yet it had no one to care for it. So, from the dust of the ground, the Creator formed a human being. Breath entered the lungs, and Adam opened his eyes to a world filled with wonder. The first breath of life was also the first moment of awe.

He walked through the garden that God had planted—Eden, a place overflowing with beauty. Rivers flowed clear as glass, animals roamed without fear, and fruit hung ripe on every tree. Each sound—the rustle of leaves, the song of birds—was part of a perfect harmony. Adam gave names to the creatures and learned their ways, but deep inside, he felt something missing.

The Creator understood and formed another—Eve—so that humanity would not walk alone. When Adam saw her, he saw reflection and belonging. Together, they tended the garden, laughed in its beauty, and walked with God in peace. There was no fear, no pain, no shame—only light and life as they were meant to be.

When the sixth day ended, the Creator rested. Not from exhaustion, but from satisfaction. The world was complete—filled with balance, beauty, and purpose. The seventh day became a pause, a holy breath that whispered, "It is good."

Even now, that same rhythm continues: light pushing back darkness, chaos finding order, hearts breathing life again. Creation isn't just a story from long ago—it's a reminder that the same voice still speaks, still creates, and still calls everything, including you, good.

What It Means

The story of creation reveals that everything began with purpose. The same power that spoke galaxies into motion shaped your life with intention. You were designed to reflect light—to bring goodness into the world.

 ### Life Lesson

Nothing about you is random. You were created with care, made to build, protect, and love in ways only you can.

 ### Try This

Spend five quiet minutes outdoors this week. Notice the details—the air, the colors, the sounds. Thank God for one thing He made that fills you with peace, and one way He made you to bring light.

 ### Did You Know?

The Hebrew word bara—"to create"—is used only when God is the subject. It means making something completely new from nothing, showing that creation wasn't crafted from chaos, but from divine imagination.

 ### Words To Know

Eden – A garden meaning "delight," the home of the first humans.
Image of God – The reflection of God's character in people through love, creativity, and freedom.
Sabbath – A sacred day of rest and joy after creation was complete.

 ### Short Prayer

Creator of all things, thank You for light that drives out darkness and for breath that fills my lungs. Teach me to see beauty in Your world and to care for what You've made. Help me live with purpose and peace today. Amen.

2 When Trust Broke — The Fall (Genesis 3)

The garden was still perfect when it happened. The air was soft and bright, filled with the scent of fruit and the sound of water moving gently through the trees. Adam and Eve lived without fear or worry. Everything they needed was within reach—food, peace, beauty, and the steady presence of God walking with them in the cool of the day.

There was only one boundary in this world of freedom. God had said they could eat from every tree except one—the tree of the knowledge of good and evil. It wasn't a cruel rule; it was an invitation to trust. To believe that love was enough, that they didn't need to define good and evil for themselves.

But one afternoon, as the light filtered through the leaves, Eve found herself near that forbidden tree. A voice spoke from its branches—quiet but sharp, twisting truth into question. "Did God really say you can't eat from any tree?" it asked.

Eve hesitated. The serpent's eyes glinted as it spoke again, its tone smooth, almost friendly. "You won't die. God just doesn't want you to be like Him—to know everything." The thought took root: maybe God was holding something back. The fruit looked beautiful, glowing in the sunlight, its promise too strong to resist. She reached out, took it, and tasted.

In that moment, something shifted inside her. The world around her didn't explode or darken—but something invisible cracked. She handed the fruit to Adam, and he ate too. Their eyes opened, and for the first time, they saw themselves differently. Innocence was gone. They felt shame, confusion, fear—emotions that had never existed before.

When they heard God walking through the garden, they hid. The Creator who had given them everything called out gently, "Where are you?" Not because He didn't know, but because He wanted them to face the truth. Adam answered, voice trembling, "I was afraid... so I hid."

Fear had entered a world that had never known it. Trust, once whole, was broken. God listened, sorrow in His voice, as He explained the consequences of what had happened. The harmony of creation was fractured—pain would now touch life, and the world would carry the weight of disobedience. Yet even in that moment, He did not abandon them. He made garments to cover their shame and promised that one day, someone would come to make things right again.

As Adam and Eve stepped out of Eden, the wind carried the scent of the garden behind them—sweet but fading. They looked back once more before walking into a world that would now know both beauty and struggle. The path forward would be hard, but the promise of redemption was already alive in God's words. Even when trust broke, love did not.

WHAT IT MEANS

This story isn't just about one mistake—it's about the human heart. We all wrestle with the same question: "Can I trust God's way more than my own?" Even when we fall, His love stays and begins to restore what's broken.

 LIFE LESSON

Real freedom isn't doing whatever we want; it's trusting the One who knows what leads to life.

 TRY THIS

Think of one area in your life where you're tempted to do things your own way. Pause and pray before acting. Ask God for wisdom to choose what brings peace instead of regret.

 DID YOU KNOW?

In Hebrew, the word Eve means "life." Even after the fall, her name remained a promise that life and hope would continue despite failure.

 WORDS TO KNOW

Temptation – The pull toward something that looks good but leads away from truth.

Grace – God's undeserved love and forgiveness that meets us even when we fail.

 SHORT PRAYER

God, thank You for loving me even when I make mistakes. Help me to trust You when I'm unsure and to choose what's right, even when it's hard. Teach me to believe that Your way is always good. Amen.

3. Jealousy at the Door — Cain + Abel (Genesis 4)

Outside the garden, life was different. The air carried dust instead of sweetness, and the ground, once generous, now demanded sweat and work. Adam and Eve built a new life, learning how to plant, harvest, and survive in a world that wasn't as easy as the one they'd lost. In time, they had two sons. The first was Cain, who became a farmer. The second was Abel, who cared for flocks of sheep. Both learned how to work the land in their own way, and both knew that their lives still depended on the Creator who had given everything breath.

One day, they each decided to bring an offering to God—a way of saying thank you, of showing love and trust. Cain gathered some crops from his field. Abel brought the best of his flock, the firstborn lambs, pure and strong.

When they placed their offerings before God, the smoke from Abel's gift rose with favor, but Cain's offering did not. The difference wasn't in what they gave, but in the heart behind it. Abel offered with faith and gratitude; Cain gave out of duty, holding back his best.

Jealousy began to coil around Cain's heart. The thought grew louder: Why him? Why not me? The more he stared at his brother, the more the anger burned. His face darkened, his chest tightened, and bitterness whispered that he had been wronged.

Then God spoke gently to him, almost like a parent to a child on the edge of a bad choice. "Why are you angry?" He asked. "If you do what is right, won't you be accepted? But if you don't, sin is crouching at your door—it wants to control you, but you must rule over it." The warning was clear: jealousy was a wild thing waiting to be let in.

But Cain turned away. One day, while the brothers were in the field, he invited Abel to walk with him. The open sky stretched wide above them, the sound of wind passing through grain. And then, without warning, Cain struck his brother down. The ground that once grew life now drank sorrow. The world grew quieter than it had ever been.

Later, God called to Cain, the same way He had once called to Adam: "Where is your brother?" Cain's reply came cold and defensive: "I don't know. Am I my brother's keeper?" But the truth could not hide. "Your brother's blood cries out to Me from the ground," God said. And Cain understood what he had done. The voice that had warned him was right—jealousy had opened the door to something he could not undo.

God's judgment was firm but not without mercy. Cain would wander the earth, unable to settle or forget, but God also placed a mark of protection on him so that no one would destroy him. Even in justice, there was compassion. The story of the first brothers became a story of warning—about the danger of envy, the power of choice, and the love that still refuses to disappear even after we fail.

As Cain walked away, the horizon stretched before him, empty yet alive with possibility. Somewhere deep within, he knew God had not erased him. The pain of what he'd done would follow him always, but so would the memory of a God who still spoke to him—even when he walked alone.

 ## What It Means

Jealousy can feel small at first, like a quiet thought—but if we let it grow, it can twist our heart. God's warning to Cain is the same to us: don't open the door to bitterness; choose love before anger takes root.

 ## Life Lesson

The success of others isn't your loss. Celebrate their light, and you'll find your own shining brighter.

 ## Try This

When you feel envy rise, stop and speak gratitude. Write down three things you're thankful for—things that are yours alone. Gratitude doesn't erase jealousy; it replaces it.

 ## Did You Know?

In Hebrew, the name Abel means "breath" or "vapor," symbolizing how fragile life is. His short life in the story reminds us how quickly jealousy can turn something sacred into something lost.

 ## Words to Know

Envy – The desire for what someone else has, which can turn joy into bitterness.

Mercy – Compassion that forgives when punishment is deserved.

 ## Short Prayer

God, help me guard my heart from jealousy. When I see others succeed, teach me to celebrate them instead of comparing myself. Give me peace with what I have and a spirit of gratitude that honors You. Amen.

4 Build What's Good — Noah + the Ark (Genesis 6–9)

The world had changed since the days of Eden. Fields were full, cities busy—but people had forgotten the One who gave them life. Violence and cruelty spread like a growing shadow. Everywhere God looked, hearts had turned hard. Yet among the noise, one man still listened.

Noah wasn't perfect, but he walked with God when almost no one else did. While others laughed at goodness and truth, Noah chose honesty and faith. One day, God spoke: the world would be washed clean. A great flood was coming—not to end life, but to begin it anew.

God told Noah to build an ark—a massive wooden vessel to hold his family and every kind of animal. It sounded impossible, but Noah didn't argue. He simply obeyed. Day after day, hammer after hammer, the sound of faith echoed across the dry ground.

People came to watch and mock, calling him foolish for preparing for something unseen. Still, Noah kept building. His faith spoke louder than words. When the ark was finished—sealed and towering—the skies began to change. Clouds gathered, animals arrived in pairs, and Noah's family entered the ark. The door closed. For seven days, silence. Then the first drop fell.

Rain became a roar. Water burst from sky and ground until mountains vanished beneath the flood. Everything that ignored God's call was swept away. But inside the ark there was light—the rhythm of water against wood, the sound of survival.

For forty days and nights, the rain fell. The ark drifted above the buried earth, warm with life—growls, chirps, laughter, prayer. Then one morning, the rain stopped. The ark rested on a mountain called Ararat. Noah released a raven, then a dove. When the dove returned with an olive leaf, hope was reborn.

When the doors opened, sunlight spilled across a new world. Noah built an altar—not to celebrate survival, but to give thanks. He had seen what happens when people destroy what's good—and how mercy restores life.

God made a promise then: never again would the world be destroyed by flood. As a sign, He set a rainbow across the sky—a bridge of color between heaven and earth. Each time the rain ends, it reminds us that after judgment comes grace, and after destruction, new beginnings. Noah's story isn't about escape—it's about building what's good, even when the world around you doesn't.

WHAT IT MEANS

Noah's faith shows that doing what's right may look strange to others, but obedience builds safety no storm can destroy. God values trust over popularity and still honors courage that stands alone.

 ### LIFE LESSON

Faith isn't proven by words—it's built day by day through choices that no one else may understand.

 ### TRY THIS

Think of one small way to "build something good" this week. It might be helping someone who's been ignored, standing up for truth, or showing kindness when it's not returned.

 ### DID YOU KNOW?

The ark was enormous—about 450 feet long, 75 feet wide, and 45 feet tall, roughly the size of a football field and a half. It had three decks and could have held over a hundred thousand animals of smaller size.

 ### WORDS TO KNOW

Ark – A huge wooden vessel God instructed Noah to build for protection during the flood.

Covenant – A promise or agreement made by God, like the one symbolized by the rainbow.

 ### SHORT PRAYER

God, help me to build what's good even when the world around me isn't. Give me courage to follow You when it's lonely and faith to trust You when I don't see the outcome. Let my life be a shelter of goodness and hope. Amen.

5 One Language, Many Plans — Tower of Babel (Genesis 11:1-9)

After the flood, the world began again. Families grew, villages formed, and soon the earth was full of life once more. Everyone spoke the same language, and for the first time since Eden, humanity moved together with one voice. It could have been a new beginning built on gratitude and unity—but something else began to take shape in their hearts: pride.

As people journeyed east, they came to a wide plain in the land of Shinar. The soil was rich, and the air dry enough to bake clay into bricks. They looked at the flat horizon and said to one another, "Let's build a city, and in it, a tower that reaches the heavens. Let's make a name for ourselves, so we won't be scattered across the earth."

Their plan sounded ambitious, even inspiring, but beneath it was a quiet rebellion. God had told them to fill the earth—to explore, create, and spread life everywhere. Instead, they wanted to stay in one place and build upward, not outward. They wanted to be remembered more than they wanted to obey.

The work began with excitement. Brick by brick, the tower climbed higher into the clouds. The people celebrated their progress, marveling at their own strength. "Look what we can do!" they said. But the higher they built, the less they remembered the One who gave them the ability to build at all. The tower became more than stone—it became a symbol of independence from God, a monument to human pride.

One morning, as the sun rose over the half-finished city, something changed. Workers began shouting directions, but suddenly no one understood each other. Their words twisted and shifted—commands turned into confusion, laughter into frustration. It was as if sound itself had broken. Friends who had spoken clearly a day before now heard only noise. The rhythm of unity fell apart.

The city froze in chaos. Bricklayers dropped their tools, architects argued, and the tower that was meant to touch heaven stood silent. The very thing that had been built to make them powerful became the place where their power failed.

God had seen their pride and scattered them across the earth, each group carrying a new language. The plain of Shinar was left behind, its tower unfinished, its name remembered only as Babel—"confusion." Yet even in this act, there was mercy. Humanity's diversity became a gift. Different languages, cultures, and lands would one day teach people to depend not on their own glory, but on grace.

The story of Babel isn't about punishment—it's about limits. It reminds us that unity without humility can lead to destruction. True greatness isn't about reaching the heavens; it's about living with hearts that remember who placed them under it.

What It Means

The people of Babel wanted fame more than purpose. God confused their language not to shame them, but to remind them that pride builds towers, while humility builds bridges.

 ### Life Lesson

Working together is powerful—but only when it's guided by gratitude, not pride.

 ### Try This

Today, notice where pride slips into your thoughts. Maybe it's in a project, a friendship, or a goal. Pause and ask: "Am I building this for myself, or to make something good for others?"

 ### Did You Know?

The word Babel comes from the Hebrew root balal, meaning "to confuse." Ancient ziggurats—tower-like temples found in Mesopotamia—may have inspired this story, showing how people often tried to build closer to the gods.

 ### Words To Know

Babel – The city where God confused human language to humble pride.

Pride – Thinking of ourselves as greater than we are, forgetting our need for God.

 ### Short Prayer

God, teach me to build with humility, not pride. Help me use my gifts to create good things that honor You and serve others. When I'm tempted to chase recognition, remind me that true greatness begins with gratitude. Amen.

6 Go—Even Without a Map — Call of Abram (Genesis 12:1-9)

The desert wind swept across the plains of Haran, carrying dust and the smell of travel. Abram stood outside his tent, looking at the horizon as the evening light turned the sky gold. Life was steady there—his flocks were healthy, his servants loyal, and his home comfortable. But something stirred within him, something that would not let him rest. Then one day, the voice of God came, clear and certain: "Go from your country, your family, and your father's house to the land that I will show you."

There was no map, no details, no visible path—just a promise. God said He would make Abram into a great nation, bless him, and make his name known for good.

Through him, all families of the earth would find blessing. It was a bold call for a man already seventy-five years old, living a quiet life. But faith doesn't measure comfort—it moves when God speaks.

Abram didn't hesitate long. He gathered his household, packed supplies, loaded animals, and set out with his wife, Sarai, and his nephew, Lot. Behind them lay everything familiar—the land of their ancestors, their friends, their security. Ahead lay only the unknown. Step by step, they left the life they knew for one that hadn't yet been revealed.

Days stretched into weeks, and the journey was not easy. The heat burned by day, and the nights were cold and silent. Dust clung to their clothes, and sometimes doubt crept into Abram's thoughts. But each time he looked at the stars scattered across the sky, something in his heart steadied. The same voice that had spoken once seemed to whisper again, "Trust Me."

When they reached the land of Canaan, Abram paused on a hill overlooking the fields and mountains. God spoke again: "To your offspring I will give this land." Abram built an altar there, stones stacked carefully, and worshiped. He didn't own the land, didn't even know exactly where he was—but his heart believed it was already promised.

As he continued traveling, Abram built more altars along the way, each one marking a moment of trust. Wherever he went, he honored God first. His life became a living journey of faith—one that didn't depend on directions, but on relationship.

Abram's story is not about a man who knew where he was going. It's about a man who decided that following God was enough reason to move. He didn't see the full picture, and he didn't need to. Every step became part of a larger promise that would one day lead to nations, to hope, and to a Savior.

Sometimes faith feels like walking into the unknown with nothing but a quiet certainty in your heart. That's what Abram did. He left the safe path to find the right one—and in doing so, became the beginning of a story that still shapes the world.

What It Means

Faith isn't built on clarity—it's built on trust. Abram followed God without a map because he believed the journey would be guided by the One who called him.

 ## Life Lesson

You don't need to know every detail before saying yes to what's right. Trust grows as you move, not before you start.

 ## Try This

Think of one area of life where you're waiting for perfect certainty. Take one small step forward this week—send that message, start that project, or offer that kindness—believing God will meet you in motion.

 ## Did You Know?

Abram's name means "exalted father," later changed by God to Abraham, meaning "father of many." His move from Haran to Canaan covered roughly 400 miles—a journey that would have taken months on foot.

 ## Words to Know

Faith – Trusting God even when the outcome isn't visible.
Promise – A commitment made by God that always brings hope, even through uncertainty.

 ## Short Prayer

God, help me to move forward even when I can't see what's ahead. Give me courage to trust You more than my fears and to remember that every step with You leads to something good. Amen.

7. A Promise with a Sign — Covenant with Abraham (Genesis 15; 17)

Years passed after Abram first set out from Haran. His tents moved across the hills and plains of Canaan, but the promise of descendants and a homeland still seemed far away. The stars were bright each night, the flocks grew, and his faith endured—but the child God had promised had not yet come. Abram was growing older, and the silence between prayers seemed longer.

One night, God spoke to him again. "Do not be afraid, Abram. I am your shield and your great reward." Abram looked toward the dark sky and answered honestly: "Lord, what can You give me, since I have no child?" The words hung in the air—half confession, half plea.

Then God took him outside and told him to look up. The night was clear, endless with light. "Count the stars," God said, "if you can. So shall your descendants be." The promise wasn't small—it was breathtaking. A nation born from one man's faith. Abram believed those words, even when nothing had changed yet. In that moment, his belief was counted as righteousness.

To seal the covenant, God asked Abram to prepare an offering. He laid out the animals as instructed, and as the sun set, a deep sleep came over him. Darkness fell, and a thick smoke and blazing fire passed between the pieces. It was a sacred symbol—God Himself confirming the promise. No words of uncertainty, no demands for proof—just divine commitment.

Time passed again, and still Abram waited. When he was ninety-nine years old, God appeared once more, repeating the promise with even greater clarity. "You will be the father of many nations," He said. And then, for the first time, He gave Abram a new name—Abraham, meaning "father of a multitude." Sarai too received a new name: Sarah, "princess," mother of nations yet unborn.

As a lasting sign of this covenant, God asked for something physical, a mark that would remind Abraham and his descendants of the relationship they shared. It was more than ritual; it was identity. God's people would carry His promise in their very flesh, generation after generation.

Abraham bowed low to the ground, overwhelmed. His body was old, his wife beyond childbearing years, yet God's promise didn't depend on logic or time. It depended only on His word. The covenant would hold because it was built on faithfulness, not perfection.

When Abraham rose, the desert wind was cool and steady. The stars that had once seemed so far away now felt close enough to touch. He didn't know how or when God's words would unfold, but he didn't need to. The covenant was more than a promise—it was the heartbeat of trust between heaven and earth.

WHAT IT MEANS

God's covenant with Abraham shows that His promises are not limited by age, time, or impossibility. Faith doesn't erase doubt—it chooses to believe even when the outcome feels impossible.

 ### LIFE LESSON

When God gives you a promise, your job isn't to control the timeline—it's to keep believing, even when the wait feels endless.

 ### TRY THIS

Write down one thing you've been waiting for. Instead of focusing on when it will happen, thank God for what He's already doing while you wait. Faith grows stronger through gratitude.

 ### DID YOU KNOW?

Changing a name in ancient times symbolized a new identity or purpose. God renamed Abram and Sarai to show that His promise would redefine who they were, not just what they had.

 ### WORDS TO KNOW

Righteousness – Being made right with God through faith, not through perfect actions.

 ### SHORT PRAYER

God, thank You for keeping Your promises even when I can't see how they'll happen. Teach me to trust Your timing and to believe that what You start, You will finish. Strengthen my faith as I wait. Amen.

8. SEEN IN THE WILDERNESS — HAGAR & ISHMAEL (GENESIS 16; 21:8-21)

The years after God's promise to Abraham stretched long. Sarah still had no child, and the waiting began to feel like silence. Each sunrise looked the same, and the hope that had once burned bright started to flicker. Sarah wondered if maybe she had misunderstood what God meant—maybe the promise was supposed to happen in a different way. So she came to Abraham with a plan that sounded practical but carried hidden pain.

"Take my servant Hagar," she said, "and have a child with her. Maybe I can build my family through her." In their culture, it was accepted, even expected, but it wasn't God's plan. Abraham agreed, and soon Hagar realized she was pregnant.

What had begun as obedience turned into rivalry.

Sarah's heart grew jealous, and Hagar, hurt and angry, ran away into the desert. The wilderness was wide and merciless. The sand burned under the sun, and Hagar's strength faded as she walked farther from everything familiar. She stopped near a spring of water, too tired to keep going. There, in the silence of her loneliness, a voice spoke. It was an angel—the first time Scripture records a messenger of God appearing to anyone—and He spoke to her by name. "Hagar, servant of Sarah, where have you come from, and where are you going?"

No one had ever asked her that before. She was a servant, a foreigner, invisible to those who made decisions for her. But now she was seen. The angel told her to return and promised that her son would become the father of many nations. She would name him Ishmael, meaning "God hears." And in that moment, Hagar gave God a name too: El Roi—"the God who sees me." In her pain, she had found not judgment, but compassion.

Years later, the story repeated itself in a harsher way. After Isaac was born to Sarah, jealousy rose again. The laughter of one child made the other seem like a mistake. Sarah demanded that Hagar and Ishmael be sent away. The next morning, Abraham packed bread and water, placed them on Hagar's shoulder, and watched her disappear into the wilderness. His heart must have ached, but he trusted God's word that Ishmael, too, would be blessed.

The journey was brutal. When the water ran out, Hagar placed her son under the shade of a bush and stepped away, unable to watch him die. Her sobs filled the emptiness, and again the voice of God came—not in anger, but in mercy. "What troubles you, Hagar? Do not be afraid. God has heard the boy crying." When she opened her eyes, she saw a well of water beside her. She lifted Ishmael and gave him to drink.

The desert that had once been her prison became the place of God's provision. Hagar's story is the story of anyone who has ever felt unseen, unwanted, or forgotten. She discovered that even in the harshest wilderness, God's eyes do not turn away. He sees the broken, the lost, the tired, and He provides what they need—not always escape, but life.

WHAT IT MEANS

Hagar's story shows that God's care isn't limited by status or circumstance. He sees every tear and hears every cry. Even when we feel invisible, His love finds us.

 ## LIFE LESSON

God's love doesn't skip the outcast or the overlooked. If He saw Hagar in the desert, He sees you too.

 ## TRY THIS

Take a quiet moment today and think of someone who might feel unseen—a classmate, neighbor, or relative. Send them a kind message or offer help. Be the reminder that they are not forgotten.

 ## DID YOU KNOW?

The name El Roi—"the God who sees me"—appears only once in the Bible. Hagar, an Egyptian servant, is the only person recorded to have given God a name.

 ## WORDS TO KNOW

Ishmael – Means "God hears," the son of Abraham and Hagar.
El Roi – A Hebrew name for God meaning "The One who sees me."

 ## SHORT PRAYER

God, thank You for seeing me even when I feel invisible. Help me remember that You notice every fear, every hope, and every cry. Teach me to see others the way You do—with compassion and care. Amen.

9 Laughter Arrives — Birth of Isaac (Genesis 21:1-7)

The desert sun had risen and set thousands of times since God first promised Abraham and Sarah a child. They had watched the stars, counted the years, and waited long enough for hope to feel like a dream half-remembered. Sarah had stopped imagining the sound of a baby's cry. She had stopped smiling when people spoke of miracles. And yet, even in her quiet disbelief, God's promise was still alive.

One morning, the camp stirred earlier than usual. Servants moved quickly, whispers spreading like wind through the tents. Sarah's time had come. The woman who had once laughed at the thought of motherhood now held her breath in awe. Pain turned to joy, and laughter—real, trembling laughter—filled the air as her son was born.

Abraham named him Isaac, just as God had said, a name that meant "he laughs." It was more than a name; it was the story of their journey written in a single word.

Sarah held Isaac in her arms, and tears slipped down her face. The lines of age, the years of waiting, the ache of wondering when—all of it melted in that moment. She looked down at the child and whispered, "God has brought me laughter, and everyone who hears will laugh with me." What had once been impossible was now breathing, sleeping, and crying in her arms.

Around them, life went on. The desert winds blew, the flocks grazed, and Abraham's people watched as the child of promise grew. Each sunrise reminded them that God's timing might not match theirs, but His word never fails. What He had spoken decades earlier had unfolded exactly as He intended—not late, not early, but right on time.

There had been doubts along the way. There had been mistakes, shortcuts, and moments when faith trembled. But God's promise had never been canceled. It had only been waiting for the right season to bloom. And when it did, the sound of laughter replaced the silence of waiting.

Isaac was more than a son; he was a symbol of God's faithfulness. Every giggle, every small step, every word he learned reminded his parents that the same God who can create stars from nothing can bring life where there seemed to be none.

Sarah's laughter that day wasn't disbelief anymore—it was pure joy, the kind that comes from realizing that God's promises are bigger than our fears. Even when we doubt, He still delights in surprising us with grace.

WHAT IT MEANS

The birth of Isaac reminds us that God keeps His promises in His own time. What feels delayed to us is often preparation in His plan, turning disbelief into joy.

 ## LIFE LESSON

When life seems silent, don't assume God has forgotten you. His promises may take time, but they never fail.

 ## TRY THIS

Think about something you've been waiting or praying for. Instead of giving up, write a short note to God thanking Him in advance, trusting that His timing is always perfect.

 ## DID YOU KNOW?

The name Isaac means "he laughs." God chose that name before his birth as both a prophecy and a reminder that joy often arrives right after disbelief.

 ## WORDS TO KNOW

Faithfulness – God's constant reliability in keeping His word.

 ## SHORT PRAYER

God, thank You for turning waiting into joy. Teach me to trust Your timing, even when I don't see how things will work out. Help me believe that laughter and hope are still possible. Amen.

10 When Love Is Tested — Abraham + Isaac (Genesis 22)

The morning was still when God spoke again. The camp was quiet, the air cool, the sound of sheep faint through the hills. Abraham rose before dawn, as he always did—but this day was different. He heard the voice he had learned to trust—the same voice that had led him from his home, promised him a son, and proved faithful through every season. But this time, the words pierced deeper: "Take your son, your only son Isaac, whom you love, and offer him as a sacrifice."

Abraham didn't argue or plead. He simply obeyed. His heart trembled, but his faith held. He had learned that obedience wasn't about understanding—it was about trusting the One who keeps

His word. He split the wood, called Isaac, and together they set out, the boy unaware of the weight that journey carried.

For three days they traveled in silence, the horizon endless. Abraham's thoughts wrestled between love and faith, the promise and the command. How could the God who gave Isaac now ask for him back? Yet Abraham believed that even if the promise seemed to die, God could bring it to life again.

Near the mountain, Abraham told his servants, "Stay here. The boy and I will go to worship—and we will come back." Those words carried more faith than anyone knew. Isaac carried the wood; Abraham carried the fire and the knife. Then came the question that pierced the silence: "Father, we have the fire and the wood, but where is the lamb?" Abraham answered, "God Himself will provide the lamb."

At the summit, Abraham built the altar. His hands were steady though his heart broke. Isaac trusted him completely and did not resist. As Abraham raised the knife, the air seemed to stop—until a voice called from heaven: "Abraham! Do not lay a hand on the boy! Now I know that you fear God, because you have not withheld your son."

Abraham froze. Behind him, a ram was caught in a thicket. He offered it in Isaac's place, and relief and awe filled the mountain. He named the place The Lord Will Provide. It became a truth engraved in his heart: God doesn't desire our pain—He desires our trust.

As they descended the mountain, Isaac safe beside him, Abraham's steps were lighter. The God who gave him everything had once again proven faithful. The test had not broken his love—it had revealed its depth.

What It Means

Faith isn't proven when life is easy—it's revealed when everything we love is placed in God's hands. Abraham's trust reminds us that surrender is not losing; it's believing that love and promise can survive the test.

Life Lesson

God never asks for trust to take something away but to give back something deeper—stronger faith and peace that can't be shaken.

Try This

Think of something or someone you hold tightly—something you fear losing. Take a quiet moment to tell God you trust Him with it. Ask Him to teach you peace through surrender.

Did You Know?

Mount Moriah, where Abraham was tested, is traditionally believed to be the same region where Jerusalem now stands—centuries later, another Father would give His Son there for the world's salvation.

Words to Know

Provision – God's act of supplying what is needed, often in unexpected ways.

Short Prayer

God, thank You for being faithful even when I don't understand Your ways. Help me trust You completely, knowing You will always provide. Teach me to love You above everything else and to walk in peace when faith feels costly. Amen.

11. A Ladder in the Dark — Jacob's Dream (Genesis 28:10-22)

The night Jacob left home, the world around him was silent except for the crunch of his footsteps on the desert path. He was running—away from his brother Esau, from the tension his own deceit had caused, from everything familiar. He carried no comfort but the clothes on his back and the guilt in his heart. The stars stretched endlessly above him, and the wilderness ahead seemed as empty as his thoughts.

When the sun set, he stopped near a lonely field of stones. With no tent, no companion, and no home to return to, Jacob lay down, resting his head on one of the rocks. The air was cold and still, and exhaustion finally pulled him into sleep.

That's when the darkness opened.

In his dream, Jacob saw a stairway reaching from earth up to heaven. Its base was set on the ground beside him, and its top disappeared into light. Angels moved up and down the steps, carrying out God's work—ascending and descending, bridging the distance between the human and the divine. At the top stood the Lord Himself, and His voice filled the space with promise.

"I am the Lord, the God of your father Abraham and the God of Isaac. The land where you lie I will give to you and your descendants. Your family will spread to the north and south, east and west, and through you, every nation on earth will be blessed. I am with you and will watch over you wherever you go."

The words washed over Jacob like light breaking into a dark room. He had run away believing he was alone, yet God had followed him into the wilderness. When he woke, the dawn was just beginning to color the sky, and the stone beneath his head felt warm, as if touched by heaven. He sat up, trembling, and whispered, "Surely the Lord is in this place, and I did not know it."

Jacob looked around at the barren land, now filled with meaning. He stood the stone upright and poured oil over it, marking it as a pillar of remembrance. Then he gave the place a name—Bethel, meaning "House of God." What had been just another patch of wilderness became holy ground.

Before he left, Jacob made a vow. "If God will be with me, protect me on this journey, and bring me safely home, then the Lord will be my God." It wasn't a deal—it was a declaration of awakening. The ladder in his dream had shown him that heaven wasn't distant, that grace could reach anyone, even a wanderer with a guilty heart.

As Jacob continued his journey, the image of that ladder stayed with him. Every star seemed to echo the same truth: no matter how far we run, God still meets us on the road. He builds bridges where we see only distance, and He turns lonely places into meeting points of mercy.

What It Means

Jacob's dream shows that God is never far, even when we've lost our way. His presence doesn't wait for perfect places or perfect people—it reaches into the wilderness of our lives.

 ## Life Lesson

You're never too far gone for God to find you. His grace can turn even your lowest moment into a place of renewal.

 ## Try This

Think about a place or situation that feels lonely or uncertain. Imagine God standing there with you. Whisper, "Surely the Lord is in this place," and let that truth quiet your fear.

 ## Did You Know?

The name Bethel means "House of God." Centuries later, it became one of Israel's most sacred sites, a symbol of divine presence in ordinary places.

 ## Words To Know

Bethel – "House of God," the place where Jacob saw the heavenly ladder.

 ## Short Prayer

God, thank You for meeting me in unexpected places. When I feel lost or ashamed, remind me that Your presence travels with me. Turn my loneliness into connection and my fear into faith. Amen.

12. When Family Hurts — Joseph's Dreams & Betrayal (Genesis 37)

The sun rose over the hills of Canaan, turning the sky gold and rose. In the distance, a young man walked toward the fields, his colorful robe gleaming in the light. His name was Joseph—the son of Jacob's old age, the favorite among twelve brothers. The robe, woven with bright threads and long sleeves, was a gift of love that became a spark.

His brothers saw it and felt the sting of comparison. Every thread reminded them of their father's unequal affection. Quiet resentment soon grew sharper. Joseph, young and confident, didn't help.

One night he dreamed they were gathering sheaves of grain, and his sheaf stood while theirs bowed. When he told them, they snapped, "Do you think you'll rule over us?" Their anger began to burn.

Soon he dreamed again—the sun, moon, and eleven stars bowing before him. When he shared it, even his father frowned, though he kept the memory in his heart.

Days later, Jacob sent Joseph to check on his brothers near Dothan. Joseph went gladly, unaware of the danger. When they saw him coming, his robe gleaming in the distance, they muttered, "Here comes the dreamer." Jealousy had turned to poison.

They seized him, tore off the robe, and threw him into a dry pit. His cries echoed, unanswered. Then a caravan of traders appeared on the horizon. "Let's sell him," one brother said. Silver coins clinked—the price of betrayal.

Dragged from the pit, Joseph was handed to strangers and carried toward Egypt. Dust rose behind him as his home and freedom faded away. He was only seventeen.

Back home, the brothers stained the robe with goat's blood and showed it to Jacob. "Do you recognize this?" they asked. Jacob's heart shattered. The robe that once meant love now carried only grief.

But the story wasn't over. Even on the road to Egypt, God was still with Joseph. The dreams that caused division were not forgotten—they were seeds for a future he couldn't yet see. His brothers' betrayal wasn't the end; it was the beginning of a journey that would one day heal the very wounds that broke them.

WHAT IT MEANS

Joseph's story reminds us that jealousy can destroy trust faster than anything else. But even when others hurt us, God's purpose still moves forward. What people mean for harm, He can turn into redemption.

 LIFE LESSON

When others betray you, don't let bitterness define you. Hold on to the belief that your story isn't finished yet.

 TRY THIS

If someone has hurt you, write their name and one good thing you can pray over them. It doesn't excuse the pain—it frees you from carrying it alone.

 DID YOU KNOW?

The journey from Canaan to Egypt was about 300 miles and would have taken Joseph roughly three weeks on foot. What began as slavery would one day lead to his rise as a leader who saved nations.

 WORDS TO KNOW

Jealousy – A feeling of resentment toward someone else's blessings or favor.

 SHORT PRAYER

God, when I'm hurt by people I love, help me remember that You never leave me. Teach me to forgive, to trust Your plan, and to believe that pain can still lead to purpose. Amen.

13 From Pit to Purpose — Joseph in Egypt (Genesis 39–41)

The road to Egypt was long, and Joseph walked it as a slave. The desert wind stung his face, and each step felt heavier than the last. He had lost his home, freedom, and family—but not his faith. Deep inside, a quiet certainty still burned: God had not left him.

In Egypt, Joseph was sold to Potiphar, an officer of Pharaoh. The house was grand, filled with incense and oil—far from Canaan's fields. Yet Joseph worked faithfully, and everything he touched seemed to prosper. Seeing this, Potiphar placed him over his entire household.

But not everyone in the house was honorable. Potiphar's wife noticed Joseph—his strength, his integrity—and tried to tempt him. Day after day she whispered, but he refused. "My master trusts me," he said. "How could I do such a thing and sin against God?" His loyalty was not just to Potiphar, but to the God who saw him even in chains.

One day, when no one was home, she caught him by his cloak. Joseph fled, leaving it behind. His choice for righteousness cost him dearly—she accused him of attacking her, and Potiphar, believing her lie, threw Joseph into prison—another pit, darker than the first.

But even there, the Lord was with him. The warden noticed Joseph's honesty and put him in charge of the other prisoners. Among them were Pharaoh's cupbearer and baker, troubled by dreams. Joseph said, "Interpretations belong to God. Tell me your dreams." He explained that the cupbearer would be restored and the baker would die—exactly as it happened. Before the cupbearer left, Joseph asked to be remembered. But once free, the man forgot.

Years passed. Then Pharaoh himself dreamed—of fat and thin cows, full and withered grain. None could explain them. That's when the cupbearer finally remembered. Joseph was brought from the dungeon, cleaned, and brought before the king.

Standing before Pharaoh, Joseph said, "It is not in me; God will give Pharaoh the answer." He revealed the meaning: seven years of abundance followed by seven of famine. Impressed, Pharaoh made Joseph second in command over all Egypt.

When plenty came, Joseph managed the harvest wisely. When famine struck, Egypt was ready. People from every land came to buy food—including, soon, the brothers who had betrayed him. But that is another story.

For now, Joseph stood on the palace balcony, looking out over the city that had once held him captive. The same God who was with him in the pit was with him in the palace. Every hardship—betrayal, loss, waiting—had shaped him for a purpose greater than he could imagine.

WHAT IT MEANS

Joseph's journey reminds us that faith doesn't protect us from hardship—it transforms it. Every trial becomes training when we trust God's plan more than our pain.

 LIFE LESSON

When life feels unfair, don't mistake delay for denial. God's timing often hides purpose you can't yet see.

 TRY THIS

Think about a time when something painful later led to good. Write it down as a reminder that the same pattern may be unfolding in ways you don't yet understand.

 DID YOU KNOW?

The title "second in command" meant Joseph was Pharaoh's vizier—the most powerful position in Egypt after the king. Historical records show viziers managed agriculture and stored grain, just as Genesis describes.

 WORDS TO KNOW

Providence – God's ability to bring good out of difficult situations.
Integrity – Choosing what's right even when no one is watching.

 SHORT PRAYER

God, thank You for staying with me through the highs and lows. When I can't see the reason for my struggles, help me trust that You're turning them into purpose. Give me patience, faith, and strength to keep walking. Amen.

14 Grace Wins — Joseph Forgives (Genesis 45; 50:15-21)

The years had changed everything. Egypt had survived the famine, and Joseph—once a slave and prisoner—now ruled as Pharaoh's most trusted official. His wisdom had saved countless lives. He wore fine linen, spoke a new language, and lived in a palace of marble and gold. But deep inside, his heart still carried the memory of home—the hills of Canaan, his father's face, and the brothers who had betrayed him.

When the famine reached Canaan, those brothers came to Egypt seeking food. They bowed before the man in charge, never realizing the ruler before them was the brother they had sold long ago. Joseph recognized them instantly.

His breath caught, not from anger, but from the rush of memories that flooded in all at once—the pit, the caravan, the years of loss. The dreams he had once shared as a teenager, the ones they mocked, were now standing right in front of him, fulfilled.

Joseph didn't reveal himself right away. Instead, he tested them, not out of cruelty but to see whether their hearts had changed. He watched how they treated one another, how they spoke of their father, how they grieved the idea of losing their youngest brother, Benjamin. The same men who had once been willing to sacrifice him now begged to protect Benjamin in his place. Their hearts, once cold, had softened. That was when Joseph could no longer hold back his tears.

He sent everyone else out of the room and broke down, his sobs echoing off the walls. The brothers stared in confusion as he said through his tears, "I am Joseph! Is my father still alive?" Fear struck them like lightning. They remembered what they had done, and guilt washed over them. But Joseph stepped closer, his face full of compassion. "Don't be afraid," he said. "Don't blame yourselves for what happened. You intended to harm me, but God intended it for good—to save many lives."

The words were more powerful than any judgment. They didn't erase the past, but they redeemed it. Joseph embraced his brothers one by one, holding the same men who had once hated him. In that moment, grace became stronger than revenge. The family that had been torn apart was made whole again.

Later, when their father Jacob died, fear crept back into the brothers' hearts. They wondered if Joseph's kindness would fade now that their father was gone. They sent him a message, begging for forgiveness once more. Joseph wept when he read it. "Don't be afraid," he told them again. "Am I in the place of God? You meant evil against me, but God used it for good." His voice was steady, not because he had forgotten, but because he had learned that grace doesn't depend on fairness—it depends on love.

Joseph's forgiveness didn't make him weak; it made him free. By letting go of bitterness, he broke the chain of pain that had followed their family for generations.

He chose mercy over memory, and that choice became the final victory of his story.

The brothers who had once sold him into slavery lived under his protection for the rest of their days. Their children grew up in safety, nourished by the very brother they had tried to destroy. Grace, it turned out, was stronger than betrayal.

 WHAT IT MEANS

Joseph's forgiveness shows that grace isn't forgetting the past—it's choosing to see God's purpose in it. When we forgive, we release ourselves from the weight of what was and open the door to what can be.

 LIFE LESSON

Forgiveness doesn't erase pain, but it heals the heart that gives it. Grace always wins over revenge.

 TRY THIS

Think of someone who's hurt you. Write a short prayer asking God to help you let go of anger. You may not feel ready to forgive—but even wanting to is the first step toward freedom.

 DID YOU KNOW?

Joseph's words, "You meant evil against me, but God meant it for good," are among the most quoted lines in Genesis. They capture one of Scripture's deepest truths: God can turn harm into healing.

 WORDS TO KNOW

Forgiveness – Releasing resentment and choosing peace instead of revenge.

 SHORT PRAYER

God, thank You for forgiving me again and again. Help me show that same mercy to others. Teach me to let go of bitterness and to trust that You can turn every hurt into something good. Amen.

Part III
Rescue &
A New Way to Live
(Exodus–Joshua)

15 Protected on the River — Moses in the Basket (Exodus 2:1-10)

The cries of newborns filled the land of Egypt, but this one was different. The Hebrew people had been enslaved for years, and the Pharaoh, afraid their numbers were growing too fast, had ordered every baby boy to be thrown into the Nile. It was a decree meant to destroy hope. Yet, one mother refused to let her child's life end in fear. She held him close, whispering prayers over the tiny boy whose name she did not yet speak aloud. For three months she hid him, quieting his cries, holding her breath whenever soldiers passed. But she knew she couldn't keep him hidden forever.

With trembling hands and unbreakable love, she wove a basket from reeds, sealing it with tar so it would float.

She laid her son inside, kissed his forehead, and set the basket among the tall grasses of the Nile's edge. Every motherly instinct screamed to hold on, but faith whispered to let go. Watching from a distance was the baby's sister, Miriam—young, brave, and wide-eyed. She kept her eyes fixed on the basket, following as the current carried it slowly downstream.

Then something unexpected happened. The Pharaoh's daughter came to the river to bathe. Her servants walked along the shore, chatting softly, when she noticed the small basket among the reeds. Curiosity drew her closer. She lifted the lid—and there he was. The baby cried, his tiny fists reaching for air, and her heart melted. Though she knew he was a Hebrew child, compassion overpowered every law written by her father. "This must be one of the Hebrew babies," she said softly, and in that moment, the story of deliverance began.

Miriam, thinking fast, ran forward and offered to find someone to nurse the baby. The princess agreed, unaware that the girl was his sister. So the child's own mother was called back to care for him, paid by Pharaoh's daughter herself. What had started in fear turned into a miracle of protection. When the boy was older, he returned to the palace and was adopted by the princess. She named him Moses, saying, "I drew him out of the water."

From a fragile basket on a dangerous river came the one who would one day stand before Pharaoh and lead a nation to freedom. His life began not with power or privilege, but with a mother's courage, a sister's quick thinking, and the quiet hand of God guiding the current. Even in a world that seemed cruel and unjust, divine purpose floated gently down the river, wrapped in reeds and hope.

What It Means

Sometimes the world feels unsafe, and doing what's right seems impossible. Yet God's protection often flows through small acts of faith—like a mother letting go, a sister stepping forward, or a stranger showing kindness. What looks risky may be the very path that leads to rescue.

 ## Life Lesson

Faith isn't always about holding tight—it's about trusting that when you release your fear, God is already steering what you've placed in His hands.

 ## Try This

Think of one worry you've been holding too tightly. Write it down and pray over it, asking God to guide it just as He guided Moses' basket. Keep that note as a reminder that surrender can be the start of peace.

 ## Did You Know?

The Nile River was central to Egyptian life—it brought water, food, and transportation. Pharaoh's command to throw infants into the Nile wasn't random; it used the very symbol of life as an instrument of fear. Yet God turned that river of death into Moses' path to life.

 ## Words to Know

Nile – the great river flowing through Egypt, vital to its people's survival.

Pharaoh – the title of Egypt's ruler, often considered divine.

Moses – means "drawn out," referring to his rescue from the river.

 ## Short Prayer

God, when life feels uncertain and the world seems dangerous, remind me that You are still in control. Give me the courage to trust You like Moses' mother did and to believe that You can bring safety and purpose out of what scares me. Amen.

16. A Voice from Fire — Burning Bush (Exodus 3)

The desert stretched endlessly, a sea of gold under the sun. Moses, once raised in Pharaoh's palace, now walked the dry hills as a shepherd, far from the noise and power of Egypt. The staff in his hand had replaced the scepter he once might have held. Each day felt ordinary—just sheep, dust, and silence. He had fled his old life after a terrible mistake, choosing exile over execution. In the wilderness, he tried to disappear, believing his story was over. But God wasn't finished with him yet.

One afternoon, as the flock grazed near Mount Horeb, Moses noticed something strange. A bush was on fire—but it wasn't burning up. The flames danced without consuming it.

Curiosity drew him closer. "I must turn aside and see this strange sight," he said to himself. As he stepped nearer, a voice called out from within the fire: "Moses, Moses!" Startled, he stopped in his tracks. "Here I am," he answered, his heart pounding.

"Do not come any closer," the voice said. "Take off your sandals, for the place where you are standing is holy ground." Moses obeyed, his hands trembling. Then the voice continued, "I am the God of your father—the God of Abraham, Isaac, and Jacob." At those words, Moses hid his face, afraid to look toward the blazing presence.

The voice spoke again, filled with compassion and power. God told Moses He had seen the suffering of His people in Egypt and heard their cries. He was ready to rescue them and bring them to a land flowing with milk and honey. Then came the impossible command: "So now, go. I am sending you to Pharaoh to bring My people out of Egypt."

Moses froze. Him? The runaway? The shepherd with no power or title? "Who am I that I should go to Pharaoh?" he asked. But God's answer was simple and life-changing: "I will be with you." It wasn't about who Moses was—it was about who God is. Still, Moses hesitated. "Suppose they ask me Your name—what shall I tell them?" And from the burning fire came the eternal reply: "I AM WHO I AM."

Those words echoed in his heart. God was not just a distant deity; He was alive, present, and unchanging. The fire did not burn out, and neither would God's promise. The shepherd who thought he was forgotten now carried a new mission—to speak for the One whose presence burns brighter than any flame.

That day, on holy ground, Moses' life reignited. He would no longer be a man hiding in the desert but a messenger of deliverance. The same God who called from the fire still calls hearts today—turning ordinary people into carriers of extraordinary purpose.

What It Means

God meets us in unexpected places—sometimes in the middle of our mistakes, fears, or routine days. The burning bush reminds us that God's presence transforms what seems ordinary into something sacred, and His call often begins where we least expect it.

Life Lesson

You don't need to be perfect or powerful for God to use you. When He calls, your weakness becomes the space where His strength shines through.

Try This

Find a quiet place this week—your room, a park, anywhere you can pause. Turn off distractions and listen. Ask, "God, what are You calling me to do right now?" Don't rush the answer. Just make space for His voice to spark something new.

Did You Know?

Mount Horeb, also called Mount Sinai, would later be where Moses received the Ten Commandments. The same mountain where God called him became the place where God revealed His law—a full-circle moment in Moses' journey of faith.

Words to Know

Horeb – another name for Mount Sinai, where God spoke to Moses.
I AM WHO I AM – God's eternal name, meaning He exists beyond time and never changes.
Holy ground – a place made sacred by God's presence.

Short Prayer

Lord, help me recognize Your voice even in the middle of my daily routine. When I feel unworthy or afraid, remind me that You are with me. Set my heart on fire for the things that matter to You, and give me courage to follow where You lead. Amen.

17 A Night of Freedom — Plagues + Passover (Exodus 7-12)

Darkness had fallen over Egypt, but not just in the sky. Pharaoh's pride had cast a shadow deeper than any night. He ruled with power and fear, refusing to free the Hebrew slaves despite Moses' message from God: "Let My people go." Time and again, Moses and his brother Aaron stood before the throne, their voices trembling yet firm. Each time, Pharaoh's heart hardened, and each time, God sent a new sign—a wake-up call that Egypt could not ignore.

First the Nile, once the nation's lifeline, turned to blood. Then frogs swarmed homes, gnats filled the air, and flies invaded every corner. Livestock fell ill, painful boils spread, and hail rained down like fire.

When the skies cleared, locusts devoured what remained of the crops, and darkness smothered the land for three full days. Still, Pharaoh clung to his power, pretending he could stand against the living God.

Through it all, God protected the Israelites. In their towns, the sun still shone, the animals stayed healthy, and the people endured with hope. Each plague wasn't just punishment—it was a reminder that no ruler, no empire, could silence God's promise. Yet one final sign would bring freedom.

Moses warned Pharaoh of the last plague: every firstborn son in Egypt would die that night, from the richest palace to the poorest home. But for the Hebrews, God gave a plan of protection. Each family was to sacrifice a perfect lamb and brush its blood on the doorframe of their house. Inside, they would eat a simple meal of roasted lamb, bitter herbs, and unleavened bread—food for travelers ready to move. They were to eat in haste, dressed for a journey, because deliverance was coming before morning.

At midnight, a heavy silence filled Egypt. Then came the cries—deep, breaking, unending. Every Egyptian household was struck with loss, while in the Hebrew homes, peace reigned under the sign of the lamb's blood. Pharaoh, crushed by grief, called for Moses and Aaron. "Go," he said at last, "and take your people. Leave Egypt and worship your God."

As dawn broke, thousands of Israelites hurried into the open air, hearts racing and hands shaking. For generations they had known only chains and labor, but that morning they walked free. The night of terror had become a night of freedom. God's presence went with them, guiding by cloud and fire. Behind them lay slavery; before them, promise.

And every year after, God's people remembered that night—the Passover—when mercy passed over their homes and turned sorrow into hope. The blood on the doors was more than a symbol of safety; it was a sign that deliverance had begun, and that God keeps His word, even when the night feels longest.

WHAT IT MEANS

The Passover shows that God's rescue always comes with both justice and mercy. The lamb's blood was a sign of trust—an act of faith that protection would come through obedience. Freedom isn't something we earn; it's something God provides when we follow His lead.

 ## LIFE LESSON

When everything seems out of control, remember that God is already writing your escape route. His timing may not match yours, but His rescue never fails to arrive right on time.

 ## TRY THIS

Think about an area of your life where you feel "stuck." Pray about it tonight, asking God to show you what step of faith He's asking you to take. Then, like the Israelites, prepare your heart to move forward when He opens the way.

 ## DID YOU KNOW?

The word Passover comes from the Hebrew Pesach, meaning "to pass over" or "to spare." Jewish families still celebrate Passover every year, remembering how God delivered them from slavery in Egypt—one of the oldest celebrations still kept today.

 ## WORDS TO KNOW

Passover – the night God protected Israel's homes marked with the lamb's blood.

Plague – a powerful disaster or sign sent by God to reveal His authority.

 ## SHORT PRAYER

God, thank You for being faithful even when life feels heavy or hopeless. Help me trust that You're leading me out of every place that keeps me bound. Give me the courage to follow You, step by step, into the freedom You've already planned for me. Amen.

18 Walk Through the Impossible — Red Sea (Exodus 14)

Freedom had finally come, yet the road ahead was far from easy. The Israelites left Egypt with joy, carrying what little they owned, led by Moses and guided by God's presence in a pillar of cloud by day and fire by night. They walked toward a promise they could barely imagine. But freedom often brings fear before peace. When Pharaoh realized his labor force had vanished, his heart turned to anger once again. He gathered his chariots—six hundred of his finest—and set out to bring the Hebrews back.

The sound of hooves thundered across the desert. As the Israelites camped by the Red Sea, they saw dust rising in the distance. Pharaoh's army was coming. Panic broke out. People screamed and turned to Moses: "Why did you bring us out here to die?

Weren't there graves enough in Egypt?" Their faith cracked under the weight of fear. Trapped between the sea and the soldiers, they saw no way out.

But Moses stood tall, staff in hand, and said words that would echo through history: "Do not be afraid. Stand firm and you will see the deliverance the Lord will bring you today." The wind began to rise, strong and strange. God's presence moved between the Israelites and the Egyptian army—a wall of cloud and fire that held the enemy back through the night. Then Moses stretched his hand over the sea, and the impossible happened.

The waters split. Walls of water rose on each side, and a dry path appeared straight through the heart of the sea. The people stared in awe, then stepped forward. Families, elders, children—each one walked through what had once been their greatest barrier. Their feet touched dry ground where moments before there had been only waves. The wind howled, but it carried the sound of hope.

As dawn broke, Pharaoh's army rushed in after them, the chariots clattering into the passage. But the Lord caused confusion among them—the wheels jammed, horses stumbled, and fear spread through the ranks. When Moses stretched out his hand again, the waters returned with a roar. The sea closed over the Egyptian army, and silence followed. On the far shore, the Israelites stood amazed. They were safe. Free at last.

Moses and the people lifted their voices in song: "The Lord is my strength and my defense; He has become my salvation." Their journey wasn't over, but their chains were gone forever. The God who parted the sea proved that no barrier—no fear, no enemy, no impossible situation—is too strong for His hand to break. Sometimes God doesn't remove the sea; He opens a path straight through it.

WHAT IT MEANS

The story of the Red Sea reminds us that God's power is not limited by what we see. When life feels trapped between fear and failure, faith means stepping forward even when you can't see the ground beneath your feet. God makes a way through what looks impossible.

 ## LIFE LESSON

Your biggest obstacle might be the very place where God shows His strength. Don't look back at what's chasing you—look ahead to the path He's opening.

 ## TRY THIS

Think about something that feels impossible right now—a goal, a problem, a change you're afraid to make. Write it down, then draw a line through it to symbolize the path God can create. Keep it somewhere you'll see it as a reminder: the way may open when you step in faith.

 ## DID YOU KNOW?

The Red Sea isn't actually red. Its name likely comes from the reddish coral and algae in its waters. In Hebrew, it's called Yam Suph, meaning "Sea of Reeds." The crossing site is debated, but the event stands as one of history's most powerful images of liberation.

 ## WORDS TO KNOW

Exodus – the great departure of the Israelites from slavery in Egypt.
Deliverance – being rescued or set free from danger or oppression.

 ## SHORT PRAYER

God, when fear surrounds me and I see no way out, remind me that You still part seas. Give me the courage to take the next step, trusting that You are already preparing dry ground beneath my feet. Lead me through the impossible. Amen.

19 Stone Words, Living Way —Ten Commandments (Exodus 19-20)

The journey through the wilderness had only begun, and the people of Israel were still learning what freedom really meant. After leaving Egypt, they camped at the foot of a mountain that rose sharp and silent from the desert—Mount Sinai. Here, God would not just rescue His people; He would teach them how to live. Freedom wasn't about doing whatever they wanted—it was about walking in a way that led to life, not chaos.

One morning, thunder rolled across the sky. Lightning flashed, and the mountain shook. A thick cloud settled over the peak as if heaven itself had come down to meet earth. The sound of a trumpet grew louder and louder until the air trembled. The people stood at a distance, afraid but awestruck.

Moses alone climbed the mountain, disappearing into the fire and cloud where God's presence burned bright.

There, God spoke words that would shape nations and hearts for generations to come. He gave Moses commandments—ten guiding truths carved on stone, but meant to be written in the human soul. They were simple yet powerful, showing how love for God and love for others form the core of every good life.

"You shall have no other gods before Me."

"Honor your father and mother."

"Do not steal, do not lie, do not kill."

Each commandment drew a line between freedom and slavery of a different kind—the slavery of greed, anger, pride, and selfishness. These were not rules meant to trap people, but a way to protect their hearts and their relationships. God wasn't demanding obedience for His sake alone; He was offering a framework for peace and goodness in a broken world.

When Moses returned to camp carrying the stone tablets, his face glowed with the reflection of God's glory. The people listened as he read the commandments aloud. They trembled but also felt a strange comfort—these weren't the commands of a cruel ruler, but the promises of a loving guide. The God who had parted the sea was now showing them how to live as His people.

From that day forward, the Ten Commandments stood as more than ancient laws. They were a mirror showing humanity its flaws, but also a map pointing toward life at its best. They called people to respect, honesty, purity, rest, and gratitude—values that still build strong hearts and strong communities. And though the words were carved in stone, their meaning was alive, meant to be carried not just in hands but in hearts.

WHAT IT MEANS

The Ten Commandments reveal God's heart for humanity: love Him fully and treat others with the same care you want for yourself. They aren't cold laws—they're directions to real freedom, guiding us toward peace with God and with each other.

 ## LIFE LESSON

True freedom isn't doing whatever you want; it's choosing what's right even when it's hard. The best boundaries don't trap you—they protect what matters most.

 ## TRY THIS

Pick one of the Ten Commandments that feels most relevant to your life right now—maybe honesty, respect, or rest. This week, focus on living it out intentionally. Notice how it changes your attitude, your peace, and your relationships.

 ## DID YOU KNOW?

God wrote the Ten Commandments with His own finger on two stone tablets—one focused on loving God, the other on loving others. The tablets were later kept inside the Ark of the Covenant, a sacred chest carried by the Israelites as a sign of God's presence among them.

 ## WORDS TO KNOW

Sinai – the mountain where God gave the Ten Commandments to Moses.

Commandment – a moral law or instruction from God.

 ## SHORT PRAYER

God, thank You for giving me a path that leads to life. Help me see Your commandments not as limits, but as gifts. Teach me to love You with all my heart and to treat others with honesty, kindness, and respect. Let Your words live in me every day. Amen.

20. Daily Bread — Manna in the Wilderness (Exodus 16)

The Red Sea was behind them, but the desert stretched endlessly ahead. The people of Israel were free, yet freedom came with hunger and exhaustion. Day after day, they walked under the burning sun, and the excitement of escape faded into complaint. "Why did we leave Egypt?" they cried. "At least there we had food!" Fear twisted their memories—slavery suddenly seemed safer than uncertainty. Moses listened to their frustration and took it to God, who was patient even with their doubt.

That evening, a strange miracle began. As the sun set, flocks of quail covered the camp, providing meat for everyone. And when the morning light rose, a thin layer of dew sparkled across the desert floor.

When it dried, it left behind something small, white, and flaky—like frost but sweet. The people stared at it, puzzled. "What is it?" they asked one another. Moses smiled. "It's the bread the Lord has given you to eat." They called it manna, which literally means "What is it?"

God gave clear instructions: gather just enough for each day—no more, no less. Some tried to store extra, but by morning it was full of worms and spoiled. Only on the sixth day could they gather twice as much so they could rest on the Sabbath. It was a daily rhythm of trust: God would provide again tomorrow. The people learned to wake up early, collect their portion, and watch as the desert floor turned golden with provision.

Every morning, manna reminded them that survival didn't depend on their strength but on God's faithfulness. It tasted like honey and sustained them for forty years. There was always enough for everyone—never too much, never too little. In a place with no crops or markets, they were fed straight from heaven's kitchen. The lesson wasn't just about food; it was about dependence. God wasn't training them to survive alone—He was teaching them to trust daily, step by step, one sunrise at a time.

Eventually, when they reached the land God had promised, the manna stopped. But the memory stayed. Each crumb of that miraculous bread told a story: that God sees, God listens, and God provides—not always in advance, but always on time.

WHAT IT MEANS

Manna teaches us that faith grows through daily trust. God often provides exactly what we need for today—not the whole plan, not tomorrow's guarantee, but enough strength, wisdom, and grace for right now.

 ### LIFE LESSON

You don't need to see the whole journey to trust the One leading you. God's provision meets you one day, one step, one prayer at a time.

 ### TRY THIS

Each morning this week, take sixty seconds before checking your phone or rushing out the door. Whisper a simple prayer: "God, give me what I need today." Then notice how He answers—through peace, help, or a small moment of joy.

 ### DID YOU KNOW?

The word manna comes from the Hebrew phrase man hu?, meaning "What is it?" The Israelites ate manna for forty years—until they entered Canaan, the land God had promised them. Scholars describe it as a sweet, flaky substance that could be baked or boiled.

 ### WORDS TO KNOW

Manna – the miraculous bread God provided for the Israelites in the wilderness.

Trust – believing that God will care for you even when you can't see how.

 ### SHORT PRAYER

God, thank You for providing what I need each day. When I start to worry about tomorrow, remind me of Your faithfulness. Help me live with peace, knowing that You will meet me again with fresh mercy every morning. Amen.

21) Walls That Fall — Joshua & Jericho (Joshua 6)

The Israelites had finally reached the edge of the land God had promised them, but one obstacle stood tall and unbreakable before them—Jericho. Its walls were massive, built to keep enemies out and fear in. Inside, the people of Jericho watched anxiously, hearing stories of Israel's escape from Egypt and the parting of the Red Sea. Outside, Joshua, now the leader after Moses, looked up at the fortress and felt the weight of the impossible. Conquering Jericho by human strength was hopeless—but Joshua knew God had never asked him to rely on that.

One evening, as Joshua stood near the city, a man appeared before him holding a drawn sword.

Startled, Joshua asked, "Are you for us or for our enemies?" The man replied, "Neither, but as commander of the Lord's army I have now come." Joshua fell to the ground in awe. God's message was clear: victory would not come through strategy or might, but through obedience.

The plan God gave Joshua made no military sense. For six days, the army was to march around the city once each day—no shouting, no attacking—just walking while priests blew trumpets made of ram's horns. On the seventh day, they were to circle Jericho seven times, and when the priests gave a long blast, everyone was to shout as loudly as they could. That was the battle plan. To the soldiers, it probably sounded foolish, but Joshua trusted God completely.

Day after day, they marched. The people of Jericho must have watched from the walls, confused and mocking. But the Israelites kept walking, one circle after another, following God's command. On the seventh day, the air was tense as they marched the seventh time around. The trumpets blared, Joshua shouted, "Shout! For the Lord has given you the city!" and the people raised their voices with all their strength. The ground trembled, the walls cracked, and then—with a thunderous crash—the mighty city of Jericho fell flat.

The people rushed in, stunned by what they saw. The walls that once symbolized fear were nothing but dust. Joshua's faith had turned silence into victory, and obedience had done what weapons never could. It wasn't the shout that brought the walls down—it was the power of God moving through a people who trusted Him enough to follow directions that made no sense.

That day, Israel learned something unforgettable: sometimes God asks you to walk, not fight. Sometimes faith means marching around your problem until He tells you to shout. And when He does, no wall—no fear, no doubt, no failure—can stand in His way.

WHAT IT MEANS

Jericho's story shows that God's victories rarely look like our plans. When we trust Him, even in confusion or waiting, He works in ways we could never imagine. Faith isn't just believing He can—it's obeying while we wait for Him to act.

 ## LIFE LESSON

Walls don't fall because you're strong—they fall because God is faithful. Your job is to keep walking even when the path feels pointless.

 ## TRY THIS

Think of something in your life that feels like a wall—a challenge you can't break through. Pray about it every day for a week. Instead of forcing a solution, ask God to show you how to trust Him while you wait for His moment to make the walls fall.

 ## DID YOU KNOW?

Jericho is one of the oldest cities in the world, located near the Jordan River. Archaeologists have found evidence of collapsed walls that match the biblical description. The number seven in the story symbolizes completion—God's perfect timing and power.

 ## WORDS TO KNOW

Jericho – a fortified city in Canaan, known for its massive walls.

 ## SHORT PRAYER

God, help me trust You when my problems seem too big to move. Teach me to walk in faith, not fear, and to obey even when I don't see results yet. Thank You for being the God who brings down walls and leads me to victory. Amen.

Part IV
Courage & Kindness
(Judges-Ruth-1 Samuel)

22 Lead Like Deborah — Deborah the Judge (Judges 4–5)

The Israelites had reached another restless chapter in their story. After years of peace, they turned away from God once again, and enemies soon rose against them. This time it was King Jabin of Canaan and his fierce commander, Sisera, who led a massive army with nine hundred iron chariots—unstoppable by human strength. The Israelites lived in fear, their roads empty, their hope fading. But in those dark years, a woman named Deborah shone like a beacon of wisdom and courage.

Deborah was both a prophet and a judge—a rare leader in a time when few women held power. She sat under a palm tree between two cities, where people came to her for guidance.

Her wisdom was known throughout Israel, but she didn't seek glory; she simply listened to God. One day, God gave her a message for a man named Barak: he was to gather ten thousand soldiers and lead them into battle against Sisera's army. Victory was promised, but only if he trusted God completely.

When Deborah told Barak the plan, he hesitated. The army they faced was too powerful, and doubt gripped his heart. "I will go," he said, "but only if you go with me." Deborah didn't flinch. "Very well," she replied, "but because of the way you are going, the honor will not be yours—the Lord will deliver Sisera into the hands of a woman." She stood beside Barak not as his shadow, but as his strength. Together they led Israel into the valley, facing the roar of chariots and the dust of war.

As the battle began, a storm broke out from heaven. Rain flooded the plain, turning the iron chariots into useless traps. The mighty army of Sisera was thrown into chaos, and the Israelites surged forward in victory. Sisera fled on foot, only to fall later at the hands of Jael, a brave woman who fulfilled Deborah's prophecy. When the battle ended, peace returned to the land.

Then Deborah sang—a song of triumph and praise that still echoes through Scripture. She celebrated not her own strength, but God's faithfulness and the courage of those who stood up when others hesitated. Her leadership wasn't about power—it was about faith, wisdom, and bold action. In a time when fear ruled, Deborah led by listening to God first and moving forward with steady confidence.

Her story reminds every generation that leadership isn't about title or status. It's about standing firm when others shrink back, using your voice for what is right, and trusting that God's plan can move through anyone—man or woman, young or old, strong or afraid.

What It Means

Deborah shows that true leadership begins with listening to God and acting in courage, not pride. Her story proves that faith and wisdom are stronger than fear, and that God can use anyone willing to say yes.

 ## Life Lesson

Leadership isn't about control—it's about courage. When you let faith, not fear, guide your choices, you inspire others to do the same.

 ## Try This

Think of one area in your life where you can "lead" with courage—at school, in your family, or among friends. Take one step this week to stand up for what's right, even if it's uncomfortable. Leadership starts with small acts of faithfulness.

 ## Did You Know?

Deborah is the only female judge mentioned in the Bible and one of the few women in ancient history known for both political and spiritual leadership. Her victory song in Judges 5 is one of the oldest pieces of Hebrew poetry ever recorded.

 ## Words To Know

Judge – a leader chosen by God to guide and protect Israel before the time of kings.

Courage – doing what's right even when it's difficult or uncertain.

 ## Short Prayer

God, give me Deborah's courage to lead with wisdom and faith. Help me to listen for Your voice before I act and to stand strong when others are afraid. Teach me that true strength comes from trusting You completely. Amen.

23 Less Is More – Gideon's 300 (Judges 6-7)

The Israelites were living in fear once again. Every year, when their crops were ready, swarms of Midianite raiders swept in like locusts—burning fields, stealing animals, and leaving behind nothing but dust and hunger. People hid in caves, praying for help, wondering if God had forgotten them. In one of those hidden places, a young man named Gideon was threshing wheat in a winepress, hoping the enemy wouldn't notice him. He didn't look like a hero—just another frightened farmer trying to survive.

Then an angel appeared and greeted him with impossible words: "The Lord is with you, mighty warrior." Gideon looked around, half expecting it to be a mistake.

"If the Lord is with us," he said, "why has all this happened?" His doubt was honest and his fear real, but God saw something deeper—a heart that could grow into courage. "Go in the strength you have," the angel said, "and save Israel from Midian's hand."

Gideon wasn't convinced. "I'm the weakest in my family," he protested. To reassure him, God gave Gideon signs—a burning sacrifice that proved His presence, a fleece that turned wet while the ground stayed dry, and then the opposite the next night. Step by step, God met Gideon's insecurity with patience. Finally, Gideon gathered an army of 32,000 men. It was a start—but God had a surprise.

"You have too many men," the Lord said. Too many? Against a massive enemy? Yet God knew that if Israel won with large numbers, they'd take credit for themselves. So He began to narrow the ranks. First, those who were afraid could go home—22,000 left. Then, at a river, God tested the remaining men by how they drank. Only 300 passed the test. Three hundred against an army so vast it was described as "thick as locusts." Gideon's odds were beyond hopeless. But that was exactly where God wanted him—relying on faith, not force.

That night, God gave Gideon one more assurance: a dream from the enemy camp itself predicting Israel's victory. Encouraged, Gideon divided his 300 men into three groups. Armed not with swords, but with trumpets, jars, and torches, they surrounded the camp. At Gideon's signal, they broke the jars, lifted their torches, and shouted, "A sword for the Lord and for Gideon!" Panic erupted below. The Midianites turned on each other in confusion, and by dawn the battle was over.

It wasn't Gideon's strength that saved Israel—it was God's power shining through weakness. From a hiding farmer to a victorious leader, Gideon learned that faith grows strongest when it has nothing left to lean on but God Himself.

WHAT IT MEANS

Gideon's story shows that God often chooses the unlikely and works through the impossible. When we feel too small, too weak, or too afraid, He reminds us that His strength is what turns fear into courage and little into enough.

 ## LIFE LESSON

God doesn't need big numbers or perfect people—He needs willing hearts. When you trust Him fully, your "not enough" becomes more than enough.

 ## TRY THIS

Think of something you feel too small or unqualified to do. Instead of giving up, pray, "God, show me how to start with what I have." Then take one bold step, trusting that He can multiply your courage just like He did for Gideon.

 ## DID YOU KNOW?

The Midianite army was so large it was described as having "camels without number." Gideon's 300 men won not through might but through surprise and faith. Their torches and trumpets created the illusion of a massive army, causing the enemy to destroy itself in panic.

 ## WORDS TO KNOW

Midianites — nomadic enemies who oppressed Israel during Gideon's time.

 ## SHORT PRAYER

God, thank You for using imperfect people to do great things. When I feel too small or scared, remind me that You are strong in my weakness. Help me walk forward in faith, believing that with You, less is always more. Amen.

24 Loyalty That Shines — Ruth + Boaz (Ruth)

The fields of Bethlehem shimmered under the sun, their golden stalks bending in the wind. But for Ruth, every handful of grain meant survival. She wasn't from Israel—she was a Moabite, a foreigner. Her husband had died, leaving her alone in a land that wasn't her own. When her mother-in-law Naomi lost everything too—her husband, her sons, her hope—Ruth could have turned back to the safety of her own people. Instead, she made a choice that would change her life and echo through history.

"Where you go, I will go," she told Naomi. "Your people will be my people, and your God my God." It was more than a promise; it was love in action.

Together they returned to Bethlehem, two widows with nothing but faith and loyalty binding them. Ruth began to gather leftover grain in the fields, as the poor were allowed to do by law. Day after day she worked from dawn to dusk, her hands rough and her back sore, but her heart steady.

In one of those fields worked a man named Boaz, a respected and kind landowner—and, though neither of them knew it at first, a relative of Naomi's late husband. When Boaz saw Ruth gleaning, he asked about her story. When he learned of her devotion to Naomi, he was moved. "I've heard what you've done for your mother-in-law," he said. "May the Lord reward you for it." From that day, Boaz made sure Ruth was protected and provided for. He told his workers to leave extra grain for her and invited her to eat with his team, treating her not as an outsider but as family.

Naomi watched everything unfold and realized that Boaz was what the law called a "kinsman-redeemer"—a man who could marry Ruth to restore her family's name and future. Following Naomi's advice, Ruth humbly approached Boaz and asked for his protection. Deeply moved by her courage and purity of heart, Boaz agreed. He took care to do everything properly, honoring both the law and Ruth's dignity. Soon, they were married, and their story became one of restoration and grace.

Their son, Obed, would one day become the grandfather of King David, and from their line would come the Messiah Himself. What began as loss ended in legacy. Ruth, the outsider who chose love over comfort, became part of God's unfolding plan for redemption. Her loyalty shone brighter than despair, proving that faithfulness, kindness, and love can rewrite even the hardest story.

WHAT IT MEANS

Ruth's story shows that loyalty and kindness can change everything. God often works through quiet faithfulness—the steady love that stays when walking away would be easier. He can turn tragedy into purpose through hearts that trust Him.

 ## LIFE LESSON

Faithfulness isn't about doing something huge—it's about showing up, loving well, and trusting God to weave something beautiful out of what feels broken.

 ## TRY THIS

Think of someone in your life who might need encouragement or support. Send a kind message, help them with something practical, or just be present. Like Ruth, let your loyalty shine in small, steady ways.

 ## DID YOU KNOW?

The story of Ruth happens during the time of the Judges—a dark, chaotic period in Israel's history. Yet Ruth's story stands out as a quiet light of hope. She became the great-grandmother of King David and one of only a few women mentioned in the genealogy of Jesus.

 ## WORDS TO KNOW

Kinsman-redeemer – a male relative with the right to protect or restore a family's inheritance.

Gleaning – collecting leftover crops from fields after the harvest.

 ## SHORT PRAYER

God, thank You for turning loss into new beginnings. Teach me to love with loyalty like Ruth and to trust You when the path feels uncertain. Help me see how even small acts of kindness can become part of something greater. Amen.

25. From Tears to Calling — Hannah & Samuel (1 Samuel 1-3)

Every year, families from across Israel traveled to Shiloh to worship and offer sacrifices to God. The dusty roads filled with voices, songs, and the sound of animals being led to the altar. Among the worshipers came a woman named Hannah. To those around her, she seemed quiet, graceful, and kind—but beneath her calm, her heart carried an ache that words could hardly reach.

She had no children. In her culture, that emptiness was more than a private sorrow—it was seen as a sign of failure, a shadow that followed her wherever she went. Her husband, Elkanah, loved her deeply and tried to comfort her, saying, "Am I not better to you than ten sons?"

But his words, though tender, could not fill the silence of a childless home. To make matters worse, his other wife, Peninnah, took every opportunity to remind Hannah of what she lacked. Each year, during the journey to Shiloh, Peninnah's taunts seemed sharper, her laughter louder.

Still, Hannah went. Year after year, she prayed through tears, through silence, through disappointment. Yet her hope refused to die. Somewhere deep inside, she believed that God still heard her—even when Heaven felt quiet.

One year, as the family finished their meal at the tabernacle, Hannah slipped away. She entered the sacred place, her heart heavy but ready to break open. Kneeling near the altar, she began to weep and pray—not with loud words, but with trembling lips that barely moved. She poured out her soul before God, every sorrow, every hope, every hidden piece of her heart. "Lord Almighty," she whispered, "if You will look on my misery and give me a son, I will give him back to You all the days of his life."

It wasn't a bargain born of desperation—it was surrender. She no longer asked for a child to complete her life; she asked for one to serve God's purpose.

As she prayed, the old priest Eli watched her from a distance. Her lips moved, but no sound came, and he mistook her grief for drunkenness. "How long will you stay drunk?" he scolded. But Hannah lifted her tear-streaked face and said softly, "I am not drunk, my lord. I was pouring out my soul to the Lord." Moved by her sincerity, Eli blessed her: "Go in peace, and may the God of Israel grant you what you have asked."

Something changed in Hannah that day. Her heart felt lighter, her steps steadier. Faith had replaced the weight of despair. And soon after, her prayer was answered. She conceived and gave birth to a son—a miracle she named Samuel, meaning "heard by God." Her tears had turned into testimony.

True to her vow, when Samuel was old enough to walk and speak, Hannah brought him to the tabernacle at Shiloh. Imagine the courage it took: the same arms that had longed to hold a child were now letting him go. She knelt beside her little boy and said, "For this child I prayed, and the Lord has granted me what I asked. Now I give him to the Lord." She kissed him goodbye, but her love did not end there. Each year, when she returned for worship, she brought Samuel a new robe, carefully stitched with love and prayer.

Under Eli's guidance, Samuel grew in wisdom and faith. The boy who once slept under the soft glow of the temple lamp learned to listen—to silence, to Scripture, to the whisper of God. One night, as he lay resting near the Ark, he heard a voice call his name: "Samuel!" Thinking Eli had called him, he ran to the priest's side. "I did not call you," Eli said. "Go back and lie down." This happened again—and again—until the old man realized the truth. "It is the Lord," he said. "When He calls again, say, 'Speak, Lord, for Your servant is listening.'"

The voice came once more, gentle yet powerful. "Samuel!" And this time, the boy answered. From that moment, God's word began to flow through him. The child born from a mother's broken prayer became the prophet through whom God would guide Israel—anointing kings, restoring truth, and carrying forward the faith of a nation.

Hannah's story began with sorrow but ended in strength. Her victory wasn't loud or public; it was quiet and eternal—the kind that reshapes generations. Through her faith and sacrifice, she gave Israel not just a son, but a messenger of God. In her, we see a truth that still stands: when you surrender your deepest longing to God, He can turn pain into purpose, and longing into legacy.

WHAT IT MEANS

Hannah teaches us that God hears every prayer, even the ones whispered through tears. Sometimes His answers don't come fast, but when they do, they carry a purpose far greater than we imagined.

 ## LIFE LESSON

Your waiting isn't wasted. God may be preparing something bigger than the answer you asked for—something that blesses others long after you.

 ## TRY THIS

If you're praying for something that hasn't happened yet, write down your prayer and date it. Keep it somewhere safe. When God answers—whether soon or years later—read it again and remember that He never forgets the cries of a faithful heart.

 ## DID YOU KNOW?

Samuel's name means "God has heard." He became one of Israel's greatest prophets and was the one who anointed both King Saul and King David. His story began not in power, but in a mother's humble faith and a child's willingness to listen.

 ## WORDS TO KNOW

Tabernacle – the portable temple where Israel worshiped before the Temple was built.

Prayer – an honest conversation with God, spoken or silent.

 ## SHORT PRAYER

God, thank You for hearing me even when I don't have the words. Teach me to trust You in the waiting and to offer back to You whatever blessings You give. Help me listen like Samuel—to recognize Your voice and follow wherever You lead. Amen.

Part V
Heart after God
(1-2 Samuel, 1 Kings)

26 Facing Giants — David & Goliath (1 Samuel 17)

The valley between the hills echoed with fear. On one side stood the army of Israel, trembling. On the other, the Philistines, led by a giant who towered nearly ten feet tall. His name was Goliath, a warrior covered in bronze armor, his spear as thick as a weaver's beam. Every morning and evening for forty days, he stepped forward, shouting insults and challenges: "Choose a man to fight me! If he wins, we'll serve you—but if I win, you serve us!" His voice rolled like thunder, and not a single soldier moved. Even King Saul, once brave, stayed silent.

Meanwhile, in a small town called Bethlehem, a young shepherd named David was watching over his father's sheep.

He was the youngest of eight sons, not a soldier, not a hero—just a boy with a sling and a heart full of songs for God. When his father sent him to deliver food to his older brothers at the battlefield, David arrived to hear Goliath's roar. He watched as grown men shrank back in fear, and something rose inside him that no one expected. "Who is this man that defies the armies of the living God?" he asked.

His brothers rolled their eyes and told him to go home, but David's courage wouldn't be silenced. He went to Saul and said, "Don't let anyone lose heart. I'll fight him." Saul stared at the boy, stunned. "You can't go against this giant—you're just a youth!" But David told him stories of lions and bears he had fought while protecting his sheep. "The Lord who rescued me then will rescue me now," he said with quiet confidence.

Saul offered David his armor, but it was too heavy. David set it aside and walked into the valley with only a sling, five smooth stones, and unshakable faith. Goliath laughed when he saw him coming. "Am I a dog, that you come at me with sticks?" he shouted. But David answered, "You come with a sword and spear, but I come in the name of the Lord Almighty." Then he ran forward, swung his sling, and released a single stone. The air fell silent as the rock struck Goliath squarely on the forehead. The giant fell face-first to the ground.

The army of Israel erupted in disbelief and joy. One boy's faith had turned fear into victory. David had faced what everyone else avoided, not because he was fearless, but because he trusted a power greater than any weapon. That day proved that courage isn't about size, strength, or status—it's about who stands with you when you face your giants. And sometimes, the smallest person in the crowd is the one God chooses to remind everyone that faith always wins.

What It Means

David's victory over Goliath shows that faith doesn't depend on physical strength or experience. God delights in using ordinary people to do extraordinary things when they trust Him completely. Courage comes not from confidence in ourselves, but in Him.

 ## Life Lesson

Your "giant" may not carry a sword, but it still taunts you with fear. Face it with faith, not panic—God is bigger than whatever stands against you.

 ## Try This

Think of one "giant" in your life—a fear, habit, or challenge that feels overwhelming. Write it down and next to it, write one truth about God's strength. This week, whenever you feel small, read that truth out loud and remind your fear who's really in charge.

 ## Did You Know?

In ancient warfare, slingers like David were skilled soldiers. Stones launched from a sling could reach speeds of over 90 miles per hour—fast enough to take down even a heavily armored warrior. David's victory was miraculous, but also strategic: God used the skills he had learned in quiet places to win a public battle.

 ## Words To Know

Philistines – a powerful people who often fought against Israel.

Goliath – a giant warrior from Gath, feared for his size and strength.

Sling – a simple weapon made of leather used to hurl stones with great force.

 ## Short Prayer

God, thank You for reminding me that no problem is too big when You are with me. Help me to face my fears with faith and to trust Your strength more than my own. Teach me to see every challenge as a chance to glorify You. Amen.

27. Mercy When You Can Win — David Spares Saul (1 Samuel 24)

The caves of En Gedi were silent except for the whisper of wind and the shuffle of soldiers searching for David. Once celebrated as Israel's hero, David was now a fugitive—hunted by the very king he had once served. King Saul, driven by jealousy and fear, had turned against him after hearing songs that praised David's victories. "Saul has slain his thousands, and David his tens of thousands." Those words burned in the king's heart. Now he roamed the wilderness with three thousand soldiers, determined to kill the young man he once loved like a son.

David and his small band of followers hid deep within one of the limestone caves, waiting for Saul's army to pass. The air was heavy, their breaths held in suspense.

Then came an unexpected sound—Saul himself entered the very cave to rest, unaware that his enemy was only a few feet away in the shadows. David's men stared at him wide-eyed, whispering, "This is your chance! God has delivered your enemy into your hands!"

David crept forward, blade in hand, his heart pounding. After years of running, here was his opportunity to end the chase, to claim the throne already promised to him by God. But as he approached Saul, a different voice stirred in his spirit—the voice of conscience, of mercy. Instead of striking, David quietly cut a small piece from Saul's robe. The king, unaware, left the cave unharmed.

When Saul was far enough away, David stepped out into the sunlight and called after him, holding up the torn piece of cloth. "My lord the king! See, I could have killed you, but I will not harm the Lord's anointed." His words echoed across the canyon, full of humility and truth. Saul turned, his eyes wide with disbelief. He looked down at his robe and realized what David had done. Tears filled his eyes. "You are more righteous than I," he said. "You have treated me well, even though I tried to harm you."

For a moment, the hunter and the hunted saw each other not as enemies, but as men—one broken by jealousy, the other guided by grace. David's restraint didn't just save Saul's life; it preserved his own integrity. He proved that true greatness isn't measured by power or revenge, but by mercy.

David walked away knowing something few warriors ever learn—that winning isn't always conquering. Sometimes victory is found in the choice to forgive, even when you have every right to strike back.

WHAT IT MEANS

David's mercy toward Saul shows that character matters more than control. Choosing forgiveness when you could take revenge is one of the most powerful ways to reflect God's heart. Mercy transforms moments of conflict into chances for grace.

 LIFE LESSON

Strength isn't proven by getting even—it's shown by holding back. The strongest person is the one who can show mercy when anger seems justified.

 TRY THIS

Think of someone who's hurt or disappointed you. Instead of planning what to say or how to "win," pause and pray for them. Forgiveness doesn't excuse what happened, but it frees your heart to move forward with peace.

 DID YOU KNOW?

The wilderness of En Gedi, where this story took place, is an oasis in the Judean desert filled with caves and waterfalls. Its name means "spring of the wild goat." Many of those caves are large enough to hide dozens of people—perfect for David's band of fugitives.

 WORDS TO KNOW

Anointed – chosen or set apart by God for a special purpose.

 SHORT PRAYER

God, help me to choose mercy when it's hardest. When I feel wronged or misunderstood, teach me to respond with grace, not revenge. Give me a heart like David's—brave enough to forgive and strong enough to wait for Your timing. Amen.

28) Dance Like No One's Watching — David's Heart for God (2 Samuel 6)

The streets of Jerusalem pulsed with life as drums echoed, horns sounded, and voices lifted in joy. After years of struggle and victory, King David was finally bringing the Ark of the Covenant—the sacred chest symbolizing God's presence—back to its rightful home. This wasn't just a military triumph; it was a moment of worship, a national homecoming for the presence of God. Soldiers, priests, and children filled the road, watching as the Ark was carried on the shoulders of the Levites. Every few steps, the procession stopped so sacrifices could be offered in gratitude.

At the center of it all was David—not standing tall in royal robes, but dancing. He leapt, spun, and shouted praises with abandon, wearing only a simple linen garment, the kind priests wore. Sweat streaked his face, but his joy burned brighter than the sun. This was no performance for the crowd; it was an offering of the heart. He didn't care about how he looked or what people might say. To him, worship wasn't about appearances—it was about presence.

As the Ark entered the city, the people cheered louder, their music filling every corner of Jerusalem. Yet not everyone shared David's joy. Watching from a palace window was his wife Michal, daughter of the former King Saul. She looked down and frowned. To her, the king's wild dancing seemed undignified, even embarrassing. When David returned home, still glowing from worship, she confronted him sharply: "How the king of Israel has distinguished himself today, going around half-dressed in front of the servants!"

David's answer came without hesitation, calm but full of conviction. "It was before the Lord, who chose me," he said. "I will celebrate before the Lord. I will become even more undignified than this if it means honoring Him." His words cut through pride and expectation. David wasn't ashamed of his joy—he knew that God saw his heart, not his clothing or composure.

That day, the Ark was placed inside the city of David, and offerings of food and blessing were given to every household. The people rejoiced, not because their king was powerful, but because their king was humble before God. David's dancing became a symbol of genuine worship—an unfiltered expression of love and gratitude that didn't need perfection to be pure.

Centuries later, his example still reminds us that faith isn't meant to be quiet or polished. Sometimes, it's loud and messy and overflowing. God delights not in performance but in authenticity—in hearts willing to celebrate His goodness with all they are.

What It Means

David's dance shows that true worship comes from the heart, not from how we appear. God values honesty and joy over formality. When our hearts are focused on Him, every act—big or small—can become an expression of worship.

 ## Life Lesson

Don't hold back your faith out of fear of what others might think. When your heart belongs to God, your joy becomes contagious.

 ## Try This

Put on your favorite worship song this week and let go of self-consciousness. Sing, dance, or just sit in gratitude—whatever helps you connect with God. Worship isn't about performance; it's about presence.

 ## Did You Know?

The Ark of the Covenant was built during Moses' time and held sacred items, including the stone tablets of the Ten Commandments. Its return to Jerusalem marked a turning point in Israel's history, symbolizing that God's presence had finally come home.

 ## Words to Know

Ark of the Covenant – the sacred chest that represented God's presence among His people.

Worship – showing love and honor to God through words, music, or actions.

Praise – expressing joy and gratitude toward God for who He is.

 ## Short Prayer

God, teach me to worship You with a free heart, unafraid of what others might think. Let my joy reflect Your goodness, and may everything I do honor You. Help me remember that true faith dances to the rhythm of Your love. Amen.

29 ASK FOR WISDOM — SOLOMON'S PRAYER (1 KINGS 3)

The kingdom of Israel had entered a new chapter. King David—the shepherd, the warrior, the poet—was gone, and his son Solomon now sat upon the throne. The trumpet blasts of celebration echoed through Jerusalem, crowds cheered, and priests lifted their hands in blessing. Yet beneath the golden crown and royal robes, Solomon's heart trembled.

He was young—brilliant, yes, but untested—and the weight of a nation now rested on his shoulders. The palace walls were still lined with memories of his father's victories and songs, and Solomon could almost hear David's voice reminding him that true greatness didn't come from strength or conquest, but from walking faithfully with God.

Solomon inherited not just power, but responsibility. He knew that armies and treasures could not secure the heart of a kingdom. What he needed was something greater—wisdom to lead with justice, compassion, and discernment.

One night, he journeyed to Gibeon, where the great bronze altar stood beneath the stars. The air was cool and still as Solomon offered a thousand burnt offerings to the Lord. The flames rose high, their glow flickering across his face—a young king kneeling before the Ancient of Days. It was an act of devotion, but even more, of surrender.

That night, as sleep overtook him, heaven opened. God appeared to Solomon in a dream and spoke words that would change everything: "Ask for whatever you want Me to give you."

Imagine that moment—no limits, no conditions, only the voice of God asking what your heart desires most. Solomon could have asked for power, long life, or endless wealth. But instead, he bowed his heart and spoke from a place of awe and humility.

"You have shown great kindness to my father, David," he said, "and now You have made me king in his place. But I am only a child and do not know how to carry out my duties. Give Your servant a discerning heart to govern Your people and to distinguish between right and wrong."

His prayer was not for himself but for others. He didn't ask for comfort or triumph, but for the wisdom to lead well—to see people as God sees them, to bring justice where confusion reigned.

God was pleased. "Since you have asked for wisdom, not riches or honor, I will give you what you asked—and more," the Lord replied. "I will make you wiser than anyone who has ever lived, and I will also bless you with wealth and honor so that no king will compare to you."

When Solomon awoke, the dawn was breaking. The light spilled into his tent like a promise fulfilled.

He knew the dream had been real—he had encountered the living God.

Not long after, his wisdom was tested. Two women were brought before him, both claiming to be the mother of the same infant. The palace court grew silent as they argued, each pleading her case. There were no witnesses, no proof—only pain and desperation.

Then Solomon spoke. "Bring me a sword," he commanded. The guards froze, but obeyed. "Cut the child in two," the king said, "and give half to each woman." Gasps filled the hall. But one woman cried out in horror, "Please, my lord, give her the baby—just don't kill him!" The other stood silent. Solomon raised his hand and declared, "Give the child to her—she is his mother."

The chamber fell silent, then erupted in awe. Word of the king's wisdom spread throughout Israel and beyond. People came from distant lands to hear his judgments, to seek his counsel, and to witness the peace and prosperity that flowed from his reign.

Yet Solomon never forgot that it all began in weakness—in the quiet of a night where he admitted he didn't have all the answers. His story reminds us that wisdom doesn't begin with knowledge, but with humility. The wisest hearts are those that listen first, seek God's guidance, and lead not for their own glory, but for the good of others.

True wisdom is more than intelligence—it's the courage to live rightly, to love deeply, and to lead with integrity. That was Solomon's legacy—and it remains the kind of greatness God still honors today.

What It Means

Solomon's story shows that wisdom begins with humility. God delights in hearts that value understanding over wealth or fame. When we ask for wisdom, we're inviting God to shape how we think, act, and love.

 ### Life Lesson

What you ask for reveals what matters most to you. When you seek wisdom above everything else, you'll find that God adds blessings you didn't even ask for.

 ### Try This

Before making an important decision this week, pause and pray Solomon's prayer: "God, give me a discerning heart." Listen quietly for His guidance. Sometimes wisdom comes as peace, clarity, or a gentle nudge in the right direction.

 ### Did You Know?

Solomon's reign became one of the most prosperous in Israel's history. He built the magnificent Temple in Jerusalem and wrote much of the Book of Proverbs, a collection of timeless wisdom still read today.

 ### Words to Know

Wisdom – the ability to make good decisions through understanding and discernment.

Discernment – spiritual insight to tell right from wrong.

 ### Short Prayer

God, thank You for offering wisdom to anyone who asks. Help me to value understanding more than success, and to lead my life with kindness and truth. Teach me to see through Your eyes and walk in Your ways every day. Amen.

Part VI
Fire & Whispers
(1-2 Kings)

30. Fire on the Mountain — Elijah vs. Prophets of Baal (1 Kings 18)

For three long years, the sky over Israel had been silent. No rain, no dew—just dust and desperation. The land cracked under the weight of drought, and the people began to forget the God who had once fed them with manna and split the sea. They turned instead to Baal, a false god of storms, hoping he would bring rain. But heaven stayed closed. In that silence, one man still listened for the voice of truth—Elijah, God's prophet.

God sent Elijah to confront the nation's idolatry and its king, Ahab, whose heart had grown cold. The challenge was simple but daring: gather all the people on Mount Carmel, along with the 450 prophets of Baal. There, God would show who was real and who was not.

The crowd gathered as Elijah stood alone on one side and the prophets of Baal filled the other. His voice rose above the murmur of the mountain: "How long will you waver between two opinions? If the Lord is God, follow Him; if Baal is God, follow him." The people said nothing—they were waiting for proof.

Elijah proposed a test. Two bulls would be prepared for sacrifice—one for Baal's prophets and one for him. They would each call on their god, and the one who answered by fire would be the true God. The prophets of Baal went first. From morning till noon, they shouted, "Baal, answer us!" They danced wildly around the altar, cutting themselves in a frenzy. Hours passed, but there was no sound—no voice, no spark, nothing. Elijah watched quietly, then called out, half in sorrow, half in challenge: "Maybe he's sleeping. Maybe he's busy. Shout louder!"

As the sun began to set, Elijah stepped forward. He repaired the Lord's altar with twelve stones, one for each tribe of Israel, and dug a trench around it. Then, to remove any doubt, he told the people to pour water over the offering—not once, but three times—until the wood and stones were soaked and the trench overflowed. When everything was drenched, Elijah lifted his hands and prayed simply, "Lord, let it be known today that You are God in Israel and that I am Your servant."

Before the last word left his mouth, fire fell from heaven. It consumed not only the sacrifice but the stones, the dust, and even the water in the trench. The people gasped and fell on their faces, crying, "The Lord—He is God! The Lord—He is God!" In that instant, the silence of heaven broke, and the truth was undeniable. The false prophets fled, and soon after, clouds began to gather. Rain finally fell, washing the land clean of drought and doubt.

Elijah stood on the mountain, the storm winds lifting his hair, his heart full of awe. He had learned that faith isn't about proving God—it's about trusting Him to reveal Himself when hearts are ready to see.

WHAT IT MEANS

Elijah's story reminds us that faith isn't built on noise or show, but on quiet trust. God's power doesn't need help to be real—it only needs hearts willing to believe. When everything else fails, His fire still falls.

 ## LIFE LESSON

Don't chase after empty things that promise power or comfort. Real strength comes from standing with God, even if you stand alone.

 ## TRY THIS

Think about something you've been trusting more than God—maybe approval, control, or success. Take a moment to surrender it in prayer. Ask God to be the fire that burns away what's false and renews what's real in you.

 ## DID YOU KNOW?

Mount Carmel overlooks the Mediterranean Sea and is known for its lush beauty—an ironic setting for a drought. The showdown between Elijah and the prophets of Baal remains one of the most dramatic moments in all of Scripture.

 ## WORDS TO KNOW

Baal – a false god worshiped by many in ancient Canaan.

Altar – a place where offerings and sacrifices were made to honor God.

 ## SHORT PRAYER

God, help me trust You even when the world around me doubts. Burn away everything false in my heart and fill me with faith that stands firm. Let my life reflect Your power and truth in every moment. Amen.

31 A Quiet Voice Still Speaks — Elijah at Horeb (1 Kings 19:1-18)

The victory on Mount Carmel had been stunning—fire from heaven, rain after years of drought, and a nation bowing in awe. But triumph can fade quickly, and fear has a way of creeping in when the applause stops. When Queen Jezebel heard what had happened to the prophets of Baal, her fury burned hotter than the fire Elijah had called down. She sent a message: "By this time tomorrow, you will be dead." The prophet who had faced down an army now ran for his life.

Elijah fled into the wilderness, exhausted and alone. Under the thin shade of a broom tree, he collapsed and whispered, "I've had enough, Lord. Take my life."

He wasn't angry—just empty. Sometimes even faith-filled hearts reach a breaking point. But God, gentle as ever, sent not judgment but rest. An angel touched Elijah's shoulder and said, "Get up and eat." Beside him lay fresh bread baked on hot stones and a jar of water. Twice the angel returned, feeding him until his strength returned. With that, Elijah began a forty-day journey through the desert to Mount Horeb—the same mountain where God had once spoken to Moses.

Inside a cave on the mountain, Elijah poured out his heart. "I have been very zealous for You, Lord," he said, "but the people have turned away. I am the only one left, and now they're trying to kill me too." His words carried both grief and loneliness. Then God invited him to step outside, promising to pass by. What followed was not what Elijah expected.

A violent wind tore through the mountains, shaking the rocks—but God was not in the wind. Then came an earthquake that split the ground beneath his feet—but God was not in the earthquake. After that, a blazing fire lit up the night—but still, God was not there. Finally, after the chaos came a sound barely louder than a whisper—a gentle breeze, a still small voice. And that was where God spoke.

Elijah wrapped his cloak around his face and stood quietly at the cave's entrance. There, in the calm after the storm, God reminded him that he wasn't alone. There were still seven thousand others who had not bowed to Baal, and his mission wasn't over. God wasn't done speaking through him—He was just teaching him to listen differently.

The lesson was subtle but powerful: God doesn't always reveal Himself in thunder and spectacle. More often, He meets us in stillness—after the noise, after the fear, when our hearts are quiet enough to hear Him. Elijah had seen fire and wind and miracles, but it was the whisper that healed his soul.

What It Means

God's presence is not always dramatic or loud. Sometimes He speaks in peace, through silence, rest, or gentle reminders. The still small voice of God is steady, personal, and full of love—it restores what fear breaks.

 ### Life Lesson

Don't expect God to always shout through miracles. Learn to find Him in quiet moments—in prayer, in nature, or in the calm after your storms. His whisper is often stronger than any thunder.

Try This

Take five minutes each day this week to sit in silence. No music, no phone, no words. Just breathe and invite God to speak to your heart. You may be surprised how His peace shows up in the stillness.

 ### Try This

Mount Horeb, also called Mount Sinai, is the same place where Moses received the Ten Commandments. Elijah's encounter there mirrors Moses's—both found God not just in power, but in presence.

 ### Did You Know?

Whisper – the quiet way God sometimes speaks to the heart.
Renewal – when strength and hope return after exhaustion or despair.

 ### Short Prayer

God, when life feels loud and my fears drown out Your voice, teach me to be still and listen. Meet me in the quiet and remind me that I am never alone. Let Your whisper calm my heart and renew my faith. Amen.

32 A SMALL JAR, BIG HOPE — ELISHA + THE WIDOW'S OIL (2 KINGS 4:1-7)

The streets were quiet as the widow walked toward Elisha's home, clutching the edges of her worn cloak. Her husband, one of the prophets who had faithfully served God, was gone—and with his death came debt. The creditors had been patient, but now they threatened the unthinkable: if she couldn't pay, they would take her two sons as slaves. She had nothing left to sell, no one left to turn to, and her heart ached with fear. Yet somewhere beneath the sorrow, a flicker of faith still burned. So she came to the prophet, desperate for help.

When she told Elisha her story, he looked at her with compassion and asked a simple question: "What do you have in your house?" She thought for a moment.

"Nothing," she said—then paused—"except a small jar of olive oil." It was a tiny thing, easily overlooked, but Elisha smiled. God often starts with small things. "Go," he said, "and ask all your neighbors for empty jars—don't ask for just a few. Then go inside with your sons, shut the door, and pour oil into all the jars."

The woman must have felt both confused and hopeful. She hurried home, sending her sons door to door, collecting every container they could find—large, small, chipped, and mismatched. When they had gathered them all, they shut the door behind them, as Elisha had said. The room was still. The widow took her small jar, tilted it over the first empty pot, and watched as golden oil flowed freely. She filled one jar, then another, and another. Her hands trembled, but the stream didn't stop.

Her sons handed her more jars, their eyes wide as the oil kept coming—smooth, steady, unstoppable. The room filled with the scent of olive and miracle. Finally, when the last jar was full, the oil stopped flowing. The woman stood silent for a moment, the reality sinking in. She had started with almost nothing, yet every vessel in her home now overflowed.

When she told Elisha what had happened, he said, "Go, sell the oil, and pay your debts. You and your sons can live on what is left." What began in desperation ended in abundance. God had turned a small jar into a lifeline, showing that no situation is beyond His care. The miracle didn't come through riches or power—it came through faith, obedience, and a willingness to pour out what little she had.

That day, a grieving widow discovered that hope multiplies when placed in God's hands. The oil ran out, but her faith never did.

What It Means

The story of the widow's oil reminds us that God can take the smallest thing and turn it into more than enough. Faith isn't about having much—it's about offering what you have and trusting God to fill the rest.

 ## Life Lesson

When you feel like you have nothing left to give, remember that God begins where your strength ends. Even a small act of faith can open the door to something miraculous.

 ## Try This

Think of one "small jar" in your life—something that feels insignificant: a skill, a bit of time, a kind word. Use it this week to bless someone else. You may find that when you start pouring, God keeps refilling.

 ## Did You Know?

Olive oil in ancient Israel was precious—it was used for cooking, medicine, light, and anointing. The widow's oil wasn't just valuable; it symbolized life and blessing. Her miracle revealed that God's provision can reach into even the most ordinary things.

 ## Words to Know

Prophet – someone chosen by God to deliver His guidance or perform His work.

 ## Short Prayer

God, help me trust You with the little I have. When I feel empty, remind me that You can fill every jar of my life with Your goodness. Teach me to keep pouring out faith, even when I don't see the miracle yet. Amen.

33. When You're Afraid — Hezekiah's Prayer (2 Kings 20; Isaiah 38)

The palace in Jerusalem was still, the air heavy with the scent of oil and incense. Curtains swayed gently in the warm breeze, carrying faint echoes of distant prayers from the temple courts. Inside the royal chamber, the once-mighty King Hezekiah lay weak upon his bed. The hands that had once built, restored, and defended now trembled beside him.

The prophet Isaiah had come earlier that day with a message that silenced every hopeful whisper in the room: "Set your house in order, for you will die and not recover." The words fell like stone—simple, certain, final. For a long moment, Hezekiah stared at the wall, his mind reeling.

The walls of the palace, once symbols of strength, now felt like a cage.

Hezekiah had been one of Judah's most faithful kings. He had torn down idols, reopened the temple, and called the nation back to worship. He had trusted God when foreign armies surrounded Jerusalem and had seen deliverance with his own eyes. But now, as sickness drained his body, all the victories of the past seemed distant, overshadowed by the weight of his mortality.

When Isaiah left, the room grew quieter still. Servants stepped softly, afraid to break the silence. Then, in the dim light, the king turned his face to the wall. There were no royal decrees, no grand speeches—only one desperate, honest prayer. "Remember me, Lord," he whispered, his voice breaking. "I have walked before You faithfully and with a whole heart."

It was not pride speaking, but longing. Hezekiah wasn't begging for more years to enjoy power or wealth—he wanted time to finish the work God had begun through him, to see his people safe, to watch worship rise again in the temple he had restored. His tears stained the pillow, each one a prayer too deep for words.

And God heard.

Before Isaiah had even left the palace courtyard, the word of the Lord came again: "Go back and tell Hezekiah, My servant—I have heard your prayer and seen your tears. I will heal you."

The prophet turned back immediately. When he entered the chamber, the air seemed to shift. Light filled the room as he spoke the words that would change everything. "Thus says the Lord: I will add fifteen years to your life, and I will deliver this city from its enemies."

To seal the promise, God gave a sign. Hezekiah, weak but wide-eyed, watched as sunlight filtered through the lattice of his window onto the palace steps.

Then, before his very eyes, the shadow began to move backward—against the laws of nature, against time itself. It was as though God had reached down and turned back the clock of heaven, reminding His servant that He rules over every hour, every heartbeat, every breath.

Days passed, and strength slowly returned to the king. He rose from his bed, his voice trembling with gratitude. The same man who had once cried out in despair now sang with joy. He wrote a psalm of thanksgiving, declaring, "The living, the living—they praise You, as I do today. You have restored me to health and let me live."

Hezekiah's story became more than a record of healing—it became a testament to the power of honest prayer. He learned that courage isn't the absence of fear; it's the choice to pray through it. His tears had not been a sign of weakness, but of faith—a faith willing to bring its pain before God.

In that quiet chamber, between sickness and song, Hezekiah discovered what every heart must learn: prayer doesn't always change God's plan, but it reveals His mercy. Sometimes God answers not with explanations, but with compassion. And when life feels fragile, when hope flickers low, Hezekiah's story reminds us that the God who turns back shadows can also turn our despair into dawn.

Scan the QR code to access the audiobook and the two "Faith Challenge" planners.

Aria Wrenley

What It Means

Hezekiah's story shows that God listens to sincere hearts. Even when fear feels overwhelming, prayer opens the door for His mercy to move. Our cries aren't signs of weakness—they're invitations for God to show His strength.

 ## Life Lesson

Fear loses its power when you bring it to God. He doesn't turn away from your tears—He turns them into hope.

 ## Try This

When you're anxious or facing bad news, write down your fear as a single sentence. Then, turn it into a prayer: "Lord, here's what I'm afraid of—help me trust You with it." Keep that note somewhere as a reminder of His promise to hear you.

 ## Did You Know?

Hezekiah ruled Judah around 700 BC and is remembered as one of its most faithful kings. Archaeologists have found a tunnel he built to bring water into Jerusalem during a siege—a testament to both his wisdom and courage in times of crisis.

 ## Words to Know

Supplication – an earnest, heartfelt plea made in prayer.

 ## Short Prayer

God, when I'm afraid and don't know what to do, remind me that You still listen. Teach me to turn fear into prayer and weakness into trust. Thank You for hearing even my quietest cries and turning them into peace. Amen.

Part VII
Stand Firm
(Esther, Jonah, Daniel, Nehemiah)

34 A Second Chance — Jonah & the Big Fish (Jonah)

The waves crashed violently against the small ship, tossing it like a leaf in a storm. Sailors shouted over the roar of the sea, each crying out to his god for help. Below deck, Jonah lay asleep, trying to escape not just the storm but the truth. He was a prophet, chosen by God to deliver a message to the people of Nineveh—a city known for its cruelty and corruption. But Jonah didn't want to go. He didn't think the people there deserved mercy. So instead of obeying, he bought a ticket on a ship sailing in the opposite direction, as if he could outrun the will of God.

Now, the storm raged because of him.

When the terrified sailors discovered Jonah's secret, they pleaded, "What should we do to stop this storm?" Jonah looked at the dark sky and the churning sea and said, "Throw me overboard, and it will calm." They hesitated, but eventually they did as he said. The moment Jonah hit the water, the sea grew still. The sailors stared in awe, realizing they had witnessed the power of the true God.

Jonah sank deep beneath the waves, expecting death—but God's mercy followed him even there. From the depths came a shadow, and before Jonah could take another breath, he was swallowed by a great fish. Inside the belly of that creature, surrounded by darkness and the sound of rushing water, Jonah finally stopped running. For three days and nights, he prayed. "In my distress I called to the Lord, and He answered me," he cried. He confessed his fear, his pride, and his disobedience. And when he surrendered, God commanded the fish to release him. Jonah was thrown onto the shore—alive, forgiven, and changed.

This time, when God said, "Go to Nineveh," Jonah went. He walked through the city, proclaiming, "Forty days more, and Nineveh will be overthrown!" To his astonishment, the people listened. From the king to the poorest worker, they repented and turned from their evil ways. Seeing their sincerity, God spared the city. Jonah, still wrestling with his emotions, couldn't understand why. "They don't deserve Your compassion," he said. But God's reply was gentle and clear: "Should I not care about this great city?"

Through Jonah's journey, God revealed something timeless—that His mercy is larger than our judgment, His patience deeper than our mistakes. Even when we run the other way, He follows with grace, not punishment. Jonah didn't just get a second chance—he learned that everyone else deserves one too.

What It Means

Jonah's story reminds us that God's love reaches farther than our failures. No matter how far we run, His mercy follows. When we turn back to Him, He doesn't just forgive—He restores and repurposes us.

 ## Life Lesson

God never gives up on you. Even when you take the long way back, His grace is waiting at every turn.

 ## Try This

Think of a time you've run from something hard or avoided doing what you knew was right. Write down what stopped you. Then pray, asking God to give you courage to face it again—with humility and trust this time.

 ## Did You Know?

Nineveh was one of the largest cities of the ancient world, located in modern-day Iraq. The "great fish" that swallowed Jonah is never called a whale in the Bible—the original Hebrew simply means "large sea creature." The story emphasizes God's mercy more than the miracle itself.

 ## Words To Know

Calling – a specific purpose or mission God gives to someone's life.

 ## Short Prayer

God, thank You for giving second chances even when I fail. Teach me to listen when You call and to trust that Your mercy is greater than my mistakes. Help me bring Your compassion to others who need it too. Amen.

35 For Such a Time — Esther Saves Her People (Esther)

In the grand palace of Persia, where marble floors gleamed and golden curtains swayed, a young woman named Esther carried a secret. Though she now wore a crown, she had once been an orphan—raised by her cousin Mordecai in a foreign land. She was Jewish, a fact she had kept hidden since being chosen as queen. Her beauty had caught the eye of King Xerxes, but it was her quiet strength and grace that won his favor. No one in the palace knew that this young queen's courage would soon determine the fate of an entire people.

One day, the king's highest official, Haman, grew furious when Mordecai refused to bow to him. Pride turned to hatred, and hatred to a plan.

Haman convinced the king to issue a decree: every Jew in the empire would be killed. The news spread like wildfire, and fear swept through the land. Mordecai tore his clothes in grief and sent a message to Esther, begging her to go before the king and plead for her people's lives. But approaching the king without being summoned was forbidden—punishable by death.

For days, Esther wrestled with fear. She hadn't been called to the king in thirty days. What if he rejected her? What if her secret was exposed? Then came Mordecai's reply, the words that would ignite her courage: "Who knows if you were made queen for such a time as this?"

Esther took a deep breath and made her choice. "If I perish, I perish," she said. She asked her people to fast and pray with her for three days. When the time came, she dressed in her royal robes and entered the throne room, her heart pounding. The king looked up, his eyes softening as he saw her. He raised his golden scepter—a sign of mercy—and said, "What is your request, Queen Esther?"

Instead of speaking immediately, Esther invited the king and Haman to a banquet. Then another. Her patience and wisdom built suspense until the moment was right. At the second banquet, she finally spoke the truth: "My king, if I have found favor in your eyes, spare my life and the lives of my people. For we have been sold to be destroyed." The room fell silent. The king demanded to know who would dare to do such a thing. Esther pointed to Haman. Rage filled the king, and justice came swiftly. The decree against the Jews was overturned, and the people were saved.

The day meant for their destruction became a day of joy and celebration. Esther's bravery not only rescued her people—it reminded them that even in exile, God was still at work through ordinary people in extraordinary moments. She had stepped into fear and found faith waiting on the other side.

WHAT IT MEANS

Esther's story shows that courage often means doing the right thing even when you're afraid. God places each of us in specific moments for a reason—and when we trust Him, even quiet voices can change history.

 ## LIFE LESSON

You may feel ordinary, but God can use your life in extraordinary ways. When the moment comes to stand up for what's right, don't let fear silence you.

 ## TRY THIS

Think of one situation where you've stayed quiet but knew you could've spoken truth or shown kindness. This week, take that step. Your courage might be the answer to someone else's prayer.

 ## DID YOU KNOW?

The name Esther means "star," a fitting symbol for someone who shone in the darkest of times. The Jewish festival of Purim still celebrates how God used her bravery to deliver her people from destruction.

 ## WORDS TO KNOW

Favor – special approval or kindness shown by someone in authority.

Decree – an official order or law issued by a ruler.

 ## SHORT PRAYER

God, thank You for placing me where I am for a purpose. When fear rises, remind me that You are with me. Give me Esther's courage to speak, to act, and to trust that even my small choices can carry Your light into dark places. Amen.

36. Lions Lose Tonight — Daniel in the Lions' Den (Daniel 6)

The kingdom of Babylon had changed rulers, but Daniel remained—a man whose wisdom and integrity shone wherever he served. Under King Darius, he rose to the highest rank, trusted more than any other official. But not everyone celebrated his success. Jealous men watched him carefully, searching for flaws. Yet Daniel's life was spotless. He worked faithfully, never using power for himself. If they were going to trap him, they realized, it would have to involve his faith.

So they devised a plan. They convinced King Darius to sign a law that no one could pray to any god or human except the king himself for thirty days. Anyone who disobeyed would be thrown into the lions' den.

The king, flattered and unaware of their scheme, sealed the decree with his royal stamp—an order that could not be undone.

When Daniel heard the law, he didn't panic or argue. Instead, he went home, opened his window toward Jerusalem, and prayed—just as he had always done. Three times a day, he knelt and gave thanks to God, even knowing that spies waited outside his door. Faithfulness, for Daniel, wasn't a reaction to comfort or safety; it was the rhythm of his life. The officials burst in and caught him in prayer, then hurried to the king. Darius was heartbroken. He admired Daniel and tried all day to save him, but the law of the Medes and Persians could not be changed.

At sunset, Daniel was brought to the den. The king's voice trembled as he said, "May your God, whom you serve continually, rescue you." The stone was rolled over the entrance, sealing Daniel in darkness. The growl of lions echoed through the pit, but Daniel's heart was steady. He prayed, not for escape, but for trust. And heaven heard.

At dawn, the king hurried back, calling out, "Daniel, servant of the living God, has your God been able to rescue you?" From within came a calm voice: "My God sent His angel, and He shut the lions' mouths. They have not hurt me." Relief and awe flooded the king's face. Daniel was lifted out unharmed, not a scratch on him. The lions, who had been instruments of fear, were silenced by faith.

King Darius then issued a new decree—this time honoring Daniel's God: "He is the living God, and He endures forever." Daniel's courage turned a kingdom's heart toward heaven. He proved that devotion doesn't depend on outcomes—it's about trust that holds steady even in the pit. That night, the lions lost, and faith won.

WHAT IT MEANS

Daniel's story reminds us that faith isn't proven by avoiding danger but by trusting God in the middle of it. Courage rooted in conviction can silence fear—and sometimes even lions.

 ## LIFE LESSON

Stand firm in your beliefs, even when pressure rises. God's presence in the den is far safer than compromise outside of it.

 ## TRY THIS

When faced with a tough decision, pause and ask yourself, "What would honor God most right now?" Choosing integrity might feel risky, but it always leads to peace that fear can't touch.

 ## DID YOU KNOW?

Archaeologists have found reliefs and texts from ancient Persia depicting lion pits used for executions, confirming the historical practice mentioned in Daniel. Lions were symbols of royal power—but in this story, God showed who truly rules over all.

 ## WORDS TO KNOW

Conviction – a firm belief that shapes choices and actions.
Deliverer – one who rescues or saves from danger.

 ## SHORT PRAYER

God, give me Daniel's courage to stay faithful no matter what surrounds me. When fear roars, remind me that You are stronger. Help me live with integrity so that others see Your power and goodness through my life. Amen.

37. Rebuild What's Broken — Nehemiah & the Wall (Nehemiah 1-6)

Far from Jerusalem, in the glittering palace of the Persian Empire, lived a man whose heart belonged somewhere else. Nehemiah served as cupbearer to King Artaxerxes—a position of immense trust, close to power, comfort, and luxury. Each day he stood before the king, tasting wine to ensure it was safe, managing court duties with quiet precision. Outwardly, his life was secure. Inwardly, he was restless.

For though his body lived among marble halls, his spirit remained among the ruins of Jerusalem—the city of his ancestors, the home of his faith. One day, travelers arrived from Judah. Nehemiah greeted them eagerly, his voice full of hope. "Tell me about home," he asked.

Their answer struck him like an arrow: "The walls of Jerusalem are broken down, and its gates have been burned with fire."

At once, all the gold and splendor around him seemed hollow. That night, Nehemiah wept. He fasted and mourned for days, unable to shake the image of a broken city once called holy. He poured out his heart before God: "Lord, the sins of our people are great—but You are faithful. Remember Your promise. Give Your servant success before this king." His prayer wasn't a plea for comfort, but a cry for purpose.

Weeks passed until one day, as he served the king, sorrow still shadowed his face. In Persia, appearing sad before the throne could cost a man his life. Yet the king noticed. "Why is your face sad, Nehemiah? You are not sick. This must be sorrow of heart."

Fear tightened his chest, but faith steadied his tongue. "How can I not be sad," he said, "when the city of my ancestors lies in ruins?"

There was a pause—the kind that feels like eternity. Then, instead of anger, came mercy. "What is it you request?" asked the king.

With a silent prayer, Nehemiah answered boldly. He asked permission to return to Jerusalem, to rebuild the city of his fathers. The king not only agreed—he sent letters for safe passage, guards for protection, and timber from the royal forests for the work ahead. God had turned the heart of an empire toward restoration.

After months of travel across deserts and provinces, Nehemiah finally arrived at Jerusalem. By night, he rode along the ruined walls, the moonlight glinting off broken stones and burned gates. The silence was heavy—like a wound that had never healed. But in that darkness, something within him stirred. The same God who had stirred his heart in the palace was now stirring a nation through him.

At dawn, he gathered the people and said, "You see the trouble we are in. Come, let us rebuild the wall of Jerusalem, so we will no longer live in disgrace." Hope flickered in weary eyes.

Slowly, hands began to lift tools. Families, priests, merchants, guards—all took their places. Shoulder to shoulder, they began the impossible.

But not everyone rejoiced. Enemies mocked them, sneering, "If even a fox climbs on it, the wall will fall." Others plotted attacks, hoping to crush their courage. Yet Nehemiah refused to bend. He set guards at the gates, armed the workers, and urged them on: "Do not be afraid. The joy of the Lord is your strength."

Day after day, they worked with one hand holding tools and the other holding weapons. Dust filled the air; sweat and prayer mingled on every face. When fear spread, Nehemiah prayed louder. When strength failed, he reminded them, "Our God will fight for us." His confidence wasn't born of power or position—it came from faith that would not break.

Fifty-two days later, against all odds, the final stone was set. The breaches were closed, the gates restored. Trumpets sounded across the city, and the people stood in awe. The same walls that had once been symbols of shame now stood as monuments of grace. Even their enemies were silenced, admitting, "This work was done with the help of God."

Nehemiah had rebuilt more than a wall—he had rebuilt a people. Those stones, raised from the ashes, became symbols of renewed identity and divine protection. Jerusalem once again had form and purpose, but more importantly, it had faith.

And as the sun set over the restored city, Nehemiah looked upon the wall and whispered a quiet prayer of thanks. The same God who had heard him in a distant palace had carried him through fear, fatigue, and opposition to this moment of triumph. It was proof that when God places a burden on your heart, He also gives the strength to see it through.

WHAT IT MEANS

Nehemiah's story shows that rebuilding always begins with prayer and persistence. When we trust God with what's broken—whether it's a city, a dream, or a heart—He gives us the strength to restore it.

 ### LIFE LESSON

When everything feels like rubble, don't quit. Start small, pray big, and keep building. God's strength turns ruins into renewal.

 ### TRY THIS

Think of one "broken wall" in your life—something that needs healing or rebuilding. This week, take one concrete step toward restoration: forgive, reach out, or start again. Trust that God can finish what you begin.

 ### DID YOU KNOW?

The walls of Jerusalem were more than two miles long and over eight feet thick in places. Nehemiah's leadership helped rebuild them in only fifty-two days—a feat historians still marvel at. His story is often cited as one of the earliest examples of effective teamwork and faith-based leadership.

 ### WORDS TO KNOW

Perseverance – steady determination to keep going despite obstacles.

 ### SHORT PRAYER

God, when I face broken things in my life, give me Nehemiah's faith to rebuild. Teach me to pray before I plan and to trust You when progress feels slow. Strengthen my hands, steady my heart, and remind me that with You, restoration is always possible. Amen.

Part VIII
God With Us
(Gospels: Birth & Early Days)

38) Hope in a Manger — Birth of Jesus (Luke 2; Matthew 1-2)

The night was quiet, and the little town of Bethlehem slept beneath a sky heavy with stars. Travelers filled every room, every inn, every corner, drawn there by an order from Caesar that everyone return to their ancestral homes for a census. Among the crowd came a young couple—Joseph, a carpenter from Nazareth, and Mary, his wife, carrying the weight of a miracle within her. The journey had been long, and by the time they arrived, Mary's time had come. Yet there was nowhere to stay. Doors were closed, rooms full. At last, someone offered a stable, a small shelter for animals, and there, in the humblest of places, the Savior of the world was born.

Mary wrapped her newborn in simple cloth and laid Him in a manger—a feeding trough for animals. There were no royal cradles or golden blankets, only straw and moonlight. Yet the air itself felt holy. God had chosen to enter the world not in power, but in tenderness, not through palaces, but through poverty. Heaven's King had come close, small enough to be held in human hands.

Outside the town, on the dark hills, shepherds kept watch over their flocks. They were ordinary men, unimportant by the world's standards. But on this night, heaven chose them first. A blinding light filled the sky, and an angel appeared. "Do not be afraid," the angel said, "for I bring you good news that will cause great joy for all people. Today in the city of David a Savior has been born to you; He is the Messiah, the Lord." Before they could speak, the night exploded with glory. A host of angels filled the sky, singing, "Glory to God in the highest, and peace on earth to those on whom His favor rests!"

The shepherds ran to Bethlehem, breathless with wonder, until they found the child just as the angel had said—wrapped in cloth, lying in a manger. They knelt beside Him, the smell of straw and sheep still clinging to their clothes, tears shining in their eyes. In that fragile baby, they saw something infinite: hope made flesh.

Far away, wise men from the east saw a new star appear and followed it across deserts and kingdoms. When they reached Bethlehem, they bowed before the child, offering gifts of gold, frankincense, and myrrh—symbols of royalty, divinity, and sacrifice. Even they, men of learning and wealth, knew they were standing before someone greater than any king of earth.

That night changed everything. The silence of centuries was broken by a baby's cry. The promise whispered through prophets and generations had finally come true. God was no longer distant—He was with us, breathing, crying, living. Hope had come, not wrapped in luxury, but in love.

What It Means

The birth of Jesus reminds us that God's light often shines from the most unexpected places. Hope doesn't arrive through power or perfection—it begins in humility, where love meets need and heaven touches earth.

 ### Life Lesson

You don't have to be perfect to experience God's presence. He meets you right where you are—quiet, messy, ordinary—and turns it into something holy.

 ### Try This

Take a few minutes in silence tonight. Think about one area of your life that feels dark or empty, and imagine Jesus bringing light into it. Whisper a simple thank-you for the hope He brings, no matter how small or fragile it feels.

 ### Did You Know?

Bethlehem's name means "House of Bread," fitting for the birthplace of Jesus, who later called Himself the Bread of Life. Shepherds near Bethlehem often tended sheep used for temple sacrifices—making it all the more symbolic that the Lamb of God was born among them.

 ### Words to Know

Messiah – the promised Savior sent by God to redeem humanity.
Incarnation – God becoming human in the person of Jesus Christ.
Redeemer – one who pays the price to rescue or restore others.

 ### Short Prayer

God, thank You for sending hope in the most humble way. Teach me to see Your presence in ordinary places and to carry Your light into a world that needs it. Let the joy of Jesus's birth fill my heart with peace and gratitude today. Amen.

39 ABOUT MY FATHER'S BUSINESS — BOY JESUS IN THE TEMPLE (LUKE 2:41-52)

Every year, families from across Israel traveled to Jerusalem for the Passover festival, a time to remember how God had freed their ancestors from slavery in Egypt. Among the crowds that filled the city streets was a boy of twelve, walking beside His parents, Mary and Joseph. His name was Jesus. The journey was long, but to Him, the temple—God's house—was worth every step. It was the center of faith, the heart of worship, and even at His young age, He felt drawn to it in a way that others couldn't quite understand.

After the festival ended, caravans of travelers began the journey home. Mary and Joseph assumed Jesus was among the group of relatives and friends traveling together. It wasn't until the end of the first day that they realized He was missing. Panic set in. They retraced their steps, hearts racing, searching the crowded streets, calling His name. For three long days they searched Jerusalem, each hour heavier than the last, until at last they found Him—sitting calmly in the temple courtyard, surrounded by teachers.

The scholars were amazed. This twelve-year-old boy listened intently, asked profound questions, and answered with wisdom far beyond His years. Mary ran to Him, relief and frustration flooding her voice. "Son, why have You treated us like this? Your father and I have been anxiously searching for You!" Jesus looked up with a steady, gentle expression and replied, "Why were you searching for Me? Didn't you know I must be about My Father's business?"

His words puzzled them, but His tone held no rebellion—only clarity. Even at twelve, Jesus knew who He was and whose purpose He served. Yet after this, He went home with Mary and Joseph, obedient and humble, growing in wisdom, stature, and favor with both God and people.

That moment in the temple wasn't just a story about a lost child found—it was a glimpse of divine calling awakening within humanity. Jesus wasn't showing off or disobeying; He was revealing that His life was already guided by His Father's plan. The same boy who sat among the teachers would one day teach nations, heal the broken, and change the world.

And for Mary and Joseph, it was a reminder that the child they raised was also the Savior they would one day follow. Even when they didn't fully understand, God's purpose was quietly unfolding, one conversation, one step, one act of obedience at a time.

WHAT IT MEANS

Jesus' time in the temple shows that God's calling often starts early and grows quietly. True wisdom isn't about age or learning—it's about knowing who you belong to and why you're here.

LIFE LESSON

When you understand your purpose, even small moments can become part of something eternal. Stay close to God, and He'll show you how to live out the mission He's placed inside you.

TRY THIS

Set aside five minutes today to reflect on what truly excites your heart in a good way—something that feels meaningful. Ask God to show you how that desire could connect with His purpose for your life.

DID YOU KNOW?

In Jewish tradition, boys at twelve began preparing for greater responsibility in faith and community life. Jesus' presence in the temple wasn't unusual—but His understanding and authority were unlike anything the teachers had ever seen.

WORDS TO KNOW

Temple – the central place of worship for the Jewish people in Jerusalem.

Obedience – willingly following what is right and honoring God through your actions.

SHORT PRAYER

God, thank You for reminding me that every stage of life has purpose. Help me listen for Your voice and learn from Jesus' example—to seek wisdom, to obey with love, and to live for You in everything I do. Amen.

40 Ready for the Mission — Baptism & Temptation (Matthew 3–4)

The Jordan River shimmered beneath the midday sun as crowds gathered along its banks. Among them stood a wild-looking man named John the Baptist, clothed in camel's hair and proclaiming a message that stirred hearts: "Repent, for the kingdom of heaven has come near!" People came from every direction, confessing their sins and being baptized as a sign of a new beginning. Then one day, a figure stepped quietly into the water—Jesus of Nazareth.

John recognized Him at once. "I need to be baptized by You," he said. But Jesus answered, "Let it be so now; it is proper for us to fulfill all righteousness."

He wasn't there to confess sin, but to identify fully with humanity—to stand in the same waters as the people He came to save. As He rose from the river, droplets sparkling on His skin, the heavens opened. The Spirit of God descended like a dove, resting on Him, and a voice thundered from above: "This is My beloved Son, in whom I am well pleased." In that moment, Jesus' mission was declared—not as a king with soldiers or a scholar with followers, but as God's Son sent to bring light into a dark world.

Immediately after that holy moment, the same Spirit led Him into the wilderness. For forty days and nights, Jesus fasted among rocks and silence, surrounded only by wind and wild beasts. Hunger gnawed at His body, but His spirit stayed fixed on the Father. Then the enemy came. "If You are the Son of God," he whispered, "turn these stones into bread." It was a challenge not of power, but of trust. Jesus answered firmly, quoting Scripture: "Man shall not live on bread alone, but on every word that comes from the mouth of God."

The devil tried again, tempting Jesus to prove Himself by leaping from the temple's height, then offering Him all the kingdoms of the world in exchange for worship. Each time, Jesus resisted—not by arguing, but by standing on truth. "Worship the Lord your God and serve Him only." His strength wasn't in power or miracles—it was in obedience.

When the devil finally left, angels came and tended to Him, and the desert winds carried the sound of victory. Jesus had passed the test. Before He healed the sick or preached a single sermon, He had already conquered the greatest battle—choosing trust over temptation.

From the river to the wilderness, His journey began with the same message that still calls to every heart: before you can change the world, you must surrender fully to God. True power begins with obedience, and every mission starts in humility.

WHAT IT MEANS

Jesus' baptism and temptation show that even the Son of God embraced humility and obedience. Real strength comes from dependence on God's Word, not from proving yourself or chasing control.

 ### LIFE LESSON

Temptation often whispers, "Take the easy way." Faith answers, "I'll trust God's way." Every victory begins with that choice.

 ### TRY THIS

When you face a hard decision, pause before reacting. Ask yourself, "Does this honor God or just please me?" Then pray for the strength to choose what's right, even when it's not easy.

 ### DID YOU KNOW?

The wilderness where Jesus fasted is a rugged region near the Dead Sea, filled with cliffs and heat. Forty days echoes Israel's forty years in the desert, showing that Jesus succeeded where humanity had failed—remaining faithful through trial.

 ### WORDS TO KNOW

Baptism – an act symbolizing cleansing, new life, and commitment to God.

 ### SHORT PRAYER

God, help me remember that strength begins with surrender. When temptation tries to lead me away from You, remind me of Your truth. Fill me with courage to follow Your way and prepare me for the mission You've designed for my life. Amen.

Part IX
Teachings & Miracles
(Gospels: Ministry)

41) Follow Me — Calling the Disciples (Matthew 4:18-22; Luke 5)

The morning sun rose over the Sea of Galilee, its golden reflection dancing across the gentle waves. Fishermen worked along the shore, mending torn nets, their hands rough from long nights on the water. Among them was Simon—better known later as Peter—along with his brother Andrew. Fishing was their life, their family's trade, the rhythm of every day. They knew the sea's moods and the scent of failure after coming back empty-handed. That morning, exhaustion clung to them like salt on their skin.

Then a stranger appeared on the shore, surrounded by a small crowd. His eyes were kind but piercing, His presence calm yet commanding. It was Jesus.

He stepped into Simon's boat and asked to be pushed out a little from the land so He could teach the people gathered on the shore. Simon obeyed, curious. The sound of Jesus' voice carried over the water, steady and full of truth—words unlike anything Simon had ever heard.

When the teaching ended, Jesus turned to Simon and said, "Put out into deep water, and let down the nets for a catch." Simon hesitated. "Master, we've worked hard all night and haven't caught anything," he replied, glancing at the empty nets. Then came the pause—the decision between doubt and faith. "But because You say so, I will let down the nets."

They cast them into the deep, and within moments the ropes strained with weight. Fish filled the nets until they began to tear. Simon shouted for help, and another boat came. Both boats overflowed, nearly sinking under the abundance. Awe flooded Simon's heart. He fell to his knees before Jesus and said, "Go away from me, Lord; I am a sinful man." But Jesus lifted him up and said, "Don't be afraid. From now on, you will fish for people."

When they reached the shore, Simon, Andrew, and the brothers James and John left everything—their nets, their boats, their livelihood—and followed Him. No questions, no negotiations, just trust. The invitation was simple but life-changing: "Follow Me."

It wasn't a call to fame or safety, but to purpose. Jesus wasn't looking for the most qualified, but for the most willing. Those fishermen would become His closest companions, witnesses to miracles and messengers of a new kingdom. What began with nets and water would spread across the world as the message of grace.

Sometimes, following Jesus means stepping away from the familiar into the unknown. But it's in that step—between fear and faith—that purpose begins to unfold.

What It Means

The disciples' calling reminds us that God often chooses ordinary people for extraordinary purposes. Following Him isn't about perfection—it's about saying yes when He calls and trusting where He leads.

 ## Life Lesson

When God invites you into something new, don't focus on what you're leaving behind—focus on who you're walking with.

 ## Try This

Take a quiet moment this week to think about one area of your life where God might be calling you to take a step of faith. It could be kindness, forgiveness, or courage. Whisper your answer: "Because You say so, I will."

 ## Did You Know?

The Sea of Galilee isn't a sea at all—it's a freshwater lake about thirteen miles long. Many of Jesus' miracles happened there, including calming the storm and walking on water. It became the backdrop for the disciples' first lessons in faith.

 ## Words to Know

Disciple – a follower or student committed to learning from a teacher's life and words.

 ## Short Prayer

God, help me to recognize Your voice when You call. Give me courage to leave behind whatever holds me back and to follow You wholeheartedly. Teach me that obedience, even in small steps, can lead to a life of purpose with You. Amen.

42. The Upside-Down Way — Beatitudes (Matthew 5:1-12)

The hillside was alive with color that morning—the deep green of the grass, the bright blue of the sky, the gentle sound of waves from the Sea of Galilee below. Crowds had begun to follow Jesus wherever He went, drawn by His miracles, but also by something deeper: His words carried peace. That day, He climbed a slope and sat down, as teachers did when they were ready to speak. The people gathered around, waiting for lessons about power or success. Instead, Jesus opened His mouth and began describing a world that turned everything upside down.

"Blessed are the poor in spirit," He said, "for theirs is the kingdom of heaven." The crowd fell silent. Poor in spirit? That wasn't what they expected.

But Jesus wasn't talking about money—He was talking about humility. Those who knew they needed God most would be the ones closest to His heart. Then came more blessings, each one surprising, almost backward to human logic. "Blessed are those who mourn, for they will be comforted." "Blessed are the meek, for they will inherit the earth." "Blessed are those who hunger and thirst for righteousness, for they will be filled."

Every sentence painted a new picture of what true happiness looked like—not in wealth, status, or control, but in compassion, mercy, and purity of heart. "Blessed are the merciful," Jesus continued, "for they will be shown mercy. Blessed are the pure in heart, for they will see God. Blessed are the peacemakers, for they will be called children of God." He was describing a kingdom where power was redefined—not as domination, but as love.

Then came the hardest part. "Blessed are those who are persecuted because of righteousness, for theirs is the kingdom of heaven." It was a promise that even in pain or rejection, those who followed God's ways would never be forgotten. The crowd listened in wonder, their ideas of blessing and success reshaped completely. The kingdom Jesus spoke of wasn't built on thrones or wealth, but on hearts transformed by grace.

When He finished speaking, the people didn't cheer or argue—they simply sat in quiet awe. Somehow, His words reached deep places in their souls, the parts that longed for meaning beyond what the world could offer. They left that hillside knowing they had glimpsed a new way to live—an upside-down way that was, in truth, right-side up in God's eyes.

WHAT IT MEANS

The Beatitudes teach that God's definition of blessing is different from the world's. He values humility, mercy, and peace more than success or comfort. True happiness begins when our hearts align with His.

 ### LIFE LESSON

Real strength is found in gentleness, and real joy in surrender. God's kingdom flips the world's values upside down—but it's there that life finally makes sense.

 ### TRY THIS

Choose one Beatitude this week—like mercy or peacemaking—and practice it intentionally. When you feel tempted to react harshly, pause and choose the upside-down way Jesus taught: kindness instead of pride.

 ### DID YOU KNOW?

The word Beatitude comes from the Latin beatus, meaning "blessed" or "happy." Jesus spoke these words from a hill near Capernaum, now known as the Mount of Beatitudes. Pilgrims still visit it today, surrounded by wildflowers and a view of the same sea He saw.

 ### WORDS TO KNOW

Meekness – strength under control; choosing gentleness instead of aggression.

Peacemaker – someone who works to bring harmony instead of conflict.

 ### SHORT PRAYER

God, help me see the world through Your eyes. Teach me to live the way Jesus described—to be humble, merciful, and full of peace. Let my life reflect Your upside-down kingdom, where love wins and true joy begins. Amen.

43   Peace in the Storm — Jesus Calms the Sea (Mark 4:35-41)

The day had been long. Jesus had spent hours teaching by the water's edge, His voice carrying over the crowds that pressed in to hear Him. As the sun dipped low, painting the horizon in gold, He turned to His disciples and said, "Let's cross to the other side." They set out in a small boat, leaving the crowd behind, the gentle rocking of the waves soothing after a day full of people and noise. Jesus, exhausted, lay down in the stern and fell asleep, His head resting on a cushion.

At first, the sea was calm, but the Galilee was known for its sudden storms. Without warning, the wind rose and the waves swelled, slamming against the boat. The disciples—experienced fishermen who knew danger when they saw it—felt panic rising.

Water poured in faster than they could bail it out. The sky turned black, the wind howled, and lightning split the darkness. They looked at Jesus, still asleep through the chaos, and fear turned to desperation. "Teacher! Don't You care if we drown?" they shouted above the storm.

Jesus opened His eyes and stood, steady even as the boat lurched beneath Him. He faced the wind, lifted His hand, and spoke words that cut through the noise: "Peace. Be still." Instantly, the storm obeyed. The wind died, the waves flattened, and the sea became as smooth as glass. The silence that followed was almost louder than the storm had been.

The disciples stared in disbelief, their hearts pounding. Jesus turned to them and asked softly, "Why are you so afraid? Do you still have no faith?" They had seen His power in miracles before, but this was different. The forces of nature itself had listened to Him. Awe filled them as they whispered to one another, "Who is this, that even the wind and the sea obey Him?"

That night on the water, they learned that peace isn't found in calm conditions—it's found in the presence of the One who commands the storm. Jesus hadn't rebuked them for waking Him; He had simply shown them that fear loses its power when faith takes its place. The same voice that spoke creation into being now spoke peace into their chaos.

Later, when life brought new storms—persecution, loss, and uncertainty—they would remember that night. The sound of the wind would no longer mean danger; it would remind them of the man who slept through the storm because He knew who held it.

What It Means

This story shows that faith isn't the absence of fear but the choice to trust God in the middle of it. Jesus doesn't promise to prevent every storm, but He promises to be present in every one.

 ## Life Lesson

Peace doesn't come from perfect circumstances—it comes from knowing that God is still in control, even when everything feels out of control.

 ## Try This

When you feel anxious or overwhelmed, take three slow breaths and whisper, "Peace, be still." Let those words remind you that Jesus is bigger than what scares you.

 ## Did You Know?

The Sea of Galilee sits about 700 feet below sea level, surrounded by hills. That geography makes it prone to sudden, violent storms—exactly the kind that caught the disciples by surprise.

 ## Words To Know

Rebuke – to speak against or correct firmly, as Jesus did to the storm.

 ## Short Prayer

God, when storms rise around me, help me remember that You are greater than my fear. Speak peace into my heart and remind me that You never leave me, no matter how rough the waves get. Amen.

44. More Than Enough – Feeding the 5,000 (John 6:1-14)

The sun was beginning to sink over the hills near the Sea of Galilee, its light spreading across the crowd that had gathered around Jesus. People had come from every nearby village—men, women, and children—drawn by His words and the miracles they'd seen. For hours, they had listened, their hunger for truth greater than their hunger for food. But now evening was coming, and stomachs were growling. The disciples looked at the sea of faces—thousands of them—and panic crept in.

Jesus turned to Philip and asked, "Where shall we buy bread for these people to eat?" It was a question that tested more than logistics.

Philip did the quick math and shook his head. "It would take more than half a year's wages to buy enough for each one to have a bite." In other words, impossible. Then Andrew spoke up, hesitant but hopeful. "There's a boy here with five small barley loaves and two fish—but how far will that go among so many?"

Jesus smiled. "Have the people sit down." The disciples obeyed, organizing the crowd across the grassy hillside. The boy stepped forward, offering his small lunch—just enough for one person, but placed in the right hands, it became limitless. Jesus took the loaves, gave thanks, and began to break them. Piece after piece, the bread multiplied. The fish did too. The disciples passed the food out, and it never ran out. Every family ate until they were full, laughter and joy replacing hunger and doubt.

When everyone had eaten, Jesus told the disciples, "Gather the leftovers, so nothing is wasted." They filled twelve baskets—more than they had started with. The miracle wasn't just in the abundance, but in the lesson: God doesn't need much to do something great. A boy's small gift became a feast because he was willing to give it.

As the crowd marveled, whispers spread that this was the promised prophet—the one sent by God. But Jesus slipped away quietly, avoiding their attempts to crown Him as king. He hadn't come to rule by force, but to reveal a kingdom that begins in the heart. That day on the hillside, He showed that with God, there's always more than enough—enough grace, enough hope, enough love to feed a world that hungers for meaning.

What It Means

This story reminds us that when we place what little we have in God's hands, He multiplies it beyond imagination. What seems small to us can become extraordinary when surrendered in faith.

 ## Life Lesson

Don't wait to have "enough" before offering what you've got. God works miracles through simple gifts given with a willing heart.

 ## Try This

Think of one thing you can share this week—your time, kindness, or talent. Offer it freely, trusting God to use it in ways you might never see.

 ## Did You Know?

The barley loaves in this story were the cheapest bread available, often eaten by the poor. The miracle's setting—on a hillside near the Sea of Galilee—mirrors how God meets people where they are, not in temples or palaces, but in everyday places.

 ## Words To Know

Abundance – the state of having more than enough; the overflow that comes from God's generosity.

 ## Short Prayer

God, thank You for being more than enough. Help me to give You what I have, even when it feels small. Teach me to trust that in Your hands, little becomes plenty, and simple acts can change lives. Amen.

45 Neighbor Means Everyone — Good Samaritan (Luke 10:25-37)

The road from Jerusalem to Jericho twisted through rocky hills and dry ravines—a lonely stretch known for danger. Travelers moved quickly through it, heads down, hoping to avoid the bandits who often hid among the rocks. One man, a Jewish traveler, wasn't so lucky. Robbers attacked him, beat him, and left him half-dead by the side of the road. The dust settled. No one came. The sun burned high.

Then, footsteps. A priest approached—the kind of man everyone expected to help. But when he saw the wounded traveler, he crossed to the other side and kept walking. Not long after, a Levite came by, another respected religious leader.

He, too, saw the man—but passed without stopping. Maybe they were afraid. Maybe they were busy. Either way, their hearts stayed closed.

Finally, a Samaritan appeared—a foreigner, part of a group despised by Jews. The two peoples avoided each other, fueled by generations of prejudice and pride. Yet when this Samaritan saw the injured man, something in him stirred. He stopped. He knelt down, poured oil and wine on the wounds to clean them, and wrapped them with strips of cloth. Then he lifted the man onto his own donkey, walked beside him to an inn, and cared for him through the night. The next morning, he gave the innkeeper money and said, "Take care of him, and when I return, I'll pay you back if the cost is more."

Days later, Jesus told this story to a lawyer who had asked, "Who is my neighbor?" expecting a neat, easy answer. But Jesus flipped the question around. "Which of these three do you think was a neighbor to the man who fell into the hands of robbers?" The lawyer replied, "The one who showed mercy." Jesus nodded. "Go and do likewise."

It wasn't just a story about kindness—it was a radical redefinition of love. The Samaritan didn't stop to ask who the man was, what he believed, or whether he deserved help. Compassion moved faster than judgment. Jesus was showing that being a neighbor isn't about proximity or similarity—it's about heart. Anyone in need is our neighbor, and love doesn't draw lines; it crosses them.

That road between Jerusalem and Jericho still runs through every human heart, where prejudice, fear, and comfort often battle compassion. The invitation remains the same: go and do likewise.

What It Means

The story of the Good Samaritan teaches that love isn't limited by boundaries or bias. True compassion means seeing need and responding, no matter who the person is.

Life Lesson

Kindness that costs you something is often the most powerful kind. Love is proven not in words, but in what you do when it's inconvenient.

Try This

Look for someone outside your usual circle who could use encouragement—a classmate, coworker, or stranger. Do one simple act of kindness this week that expects nothing in return.

Did You Know?

Jews and Samaritans in Jesus' time had a deep cultural divide that went back centuries. By choosing a Samaritan as the hero of His story, Jesus directly challenged the prejudices of His audience.

Words To Know

Compassion – deep care that moves you to take action for someone else's good.

Short Prayer

God, open my eyes to the people who need love around me. Help me to see beyond differences and show kindness that reflects Your heart. Teach me to be a true neighbor—one who acts with compassion, even when it's hard. Amen.

46 You Can Always Come Home — Prodigal Son (Luke 15:11-32)

There was once a man with two sons. The younger one grew restless, tired of rules, tired of routine. One day he came to his father and said words that must have stung: "Father, give me my share of the inheritance now." It was like saying, I want what's yours, but not you. Still, the father agreed. He divided his estate, and the younger son left home with pockets full of money and a heart chasing freedom.

He traveled far away, living fast and spending freely. For a while, it felt like happiness—friends, laughter, and no one to tell him what to do. But money disappears faster than wisdom grows.

When the last coin was gone and famine hit the land, his so-called friends vanished too. Hungry and alone, he found work feeding pigs—an unthinkable job for a Jewish man. He grew so desperate he longed to eat the pods he fed the animals. That's when it hit him: the servants in his father's house lived better than this.

So he made a decision that took more courage than leaving ever had—he turned back. As he walked the long road home, he rehearsed his apology: "Father, I've sinned against heaven and against you. I'm no longer worthy to be called your son. Make me like one of your hired servants." Dust clung to his feet, shame weighed on his shoulders, and he wondered whether his father would even look at him again.

But before he could reach the gate, his father saw him coming. He'd been watching that road for a long time. Without hesitation, the father ran—ran to his broken son, arms open, tears falling. Before the boy could finish his apology, his father wrapped him in an embrace. "Quick!" the father called to his servants. "Bring the best robe, a ring for his finger, sandals for his feet. Prepare the feast! My son was dead and is alive again; he was lost and is found."

The celebration filled the house with music and joy, but not everyone was happy. The older brother stood outside, angry. He'd stayed, worked hard, followed every rule—and now this reckless brother was being honored? When the father came out to invite him in, the older son said bitterly, "I've served you all these years and never disobeyed, yet you've never thrown a party for me." The father's answer was gentle but piercing: "My son, you are always with me, and everything I have is yours. But we had to celebrate—your brother was lost and now is found."

The younger son learned that forgiveness runs faster than failure. The older son learned that grace is not a competition. And the father's love—steady, extravagant, and unearned—showed that no matter how far you wander, the road home is never closed.

WHAT IT MEANS

The parable of the prodigal son reveals the heart of God—a Father who doesn't wait for perfect apologies, but runs to embrace us the moment we turn back. His grace never runs out, no matter how far we've gone.

 ## LIFE LESSON

You can't outdistance God's love. The moment you take one step toward Him, He's already running to meet you.

 ## TRY THIS

If there's something in your life that makes you feel far from God, talk to Him honestly about it tonight. Don't hide—just come as you are. His arms are always open.

 ## DID YOU KNOW?

In Jesus' culture, a father running to a son was shocking—grown men didn't run in public. By including that detail, Jesus showed just how radical and tender God's love truly is.

 ## WORDS TO KNOW

Repentance – turning away from mistakes or sin and returning toward God with a humble heart.

 ## SHORT PRAYER

God, thank You for welcoming me back every time I wander. Help me to trust Your grace more than my guilt and to remember that Your love never stops chasing me. Teach me to forgive others the same way You forgive me. Amen.

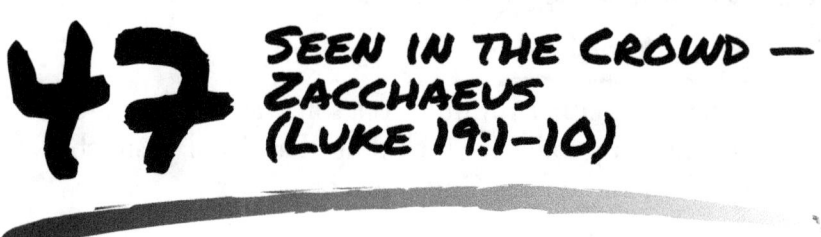

47 Seen in the Crowd — Zacchaeus (Luke 19:1-10)

The streets of Jericho buzzed with noise as Jesus entered the city. People crowded the narrow lanes, pressing close, each one eager to catch a glimpse of the teacher everyone was talking about. Word had spread about His miracles—blind eyes opened, broken lives restored—and no one wanted to miss Him. Among the crowd was a man named Zacchaeus, but unlike the others, he wasn't just curious. He was desperate.

Zacchaeus was the chief tax collector, a man who had grown rich by taking from others. His neighbors hated him, calling him a traitor for serving the Roman Empire and cheating his own people. He was powerful, but lonely; wealthy, but empty. Something about Jesus stirred a hope he hadn't felt in years.

He tried to see over the crowd, but he was short and couldn't get through. So, like a child, he ran ahead and climbed a sycamore tree, his fine robes catching on the branches as he perched among the leaves. From there, he could finally see.

As Jesus passed beneath the tree, the crowd's noise softened. Then, to Zacchaeus' astonishment, Jesus stopped. He looked up, meeting Zacchaeus' eyes as if He'd been searching for him all along. "Zacchaeus," He said, calling him by name, "come down immediately. I must stay at your house today." Gasps rippled through the crowd. Of all people, why him? A sinner, a thief? But Jesus didn't avoid brokenness—He walked straight into it.

Zacchaeus scrambled down, his heart pounding, his soul already shifting. As they walked together, whispers followed: "He's gone to be the guest of a sinner." But by the time they reached his house, something in Zacchaeus had changed. Standing before Jesus, he said, "Lord, here and now I give half of my possessions to the poor, and if I've cheated anyone, I'll pay back four times the amount." Grace had done what guilt never could—it transformed him.

Jesus smiled, His voice warm with joy. "Today salvation has come to this house," He said. "For the Son of Man came to seek and to save the lost."

That day, Jericho saw what mercy looks like when it takes a name and sits down at a table. Zacchaeus had spent his life trying to climb higher—in status, wealth, control—but it was only when he climbed down that he found what he'd been looking for.

What It Means

Zacchaeus' story shows that no one is too far gone for God to notice. Jesus sees us not for what we've done, but for who we can become when grace meets our heart.

 ## Life Lesson

You don't have to clean up your life before coming to God—just come down from whatever tree you've climbed to hide, and let Him in.

 ## Try This

Think about an area of your life you've been keeping out of God's reach—something you're ashamed of or afraid to face. This week, talk honestly with Him about it. Grace can begin the moment you stop hiding.

 ## Did You Know?

Tax collectors in Jesus' time were often Jews working for the Roman government, collecting high taxes and pocketing extra for themselves. Climbing a sycamore tree, with its wide branches, would have been both easy and undignified—showing how eager Zacchaeus was to see Jesus.

 ## Words to Know

Restoration – the act of making something whole again after it's been broken or lost.

 ## Short Prayer

God, thank You for seeing me even when I feel invisible. Help me to welcome You into every part of my life, trusting that Your grace can restore what's been broken. Teach me to live with the same mercy You've shown me. Amen.

Part X
Cross, Empty Tomb & New Start (Gospels–Acts)

48 Served at the Table — Last Supper & Gethsemane (Luke 22; John 13)

The upper room glowed softly in the lamplight as Jesus and His disciples gathered around a long, low table. It was Passover—the night when Israel remembered how God had freed their ancestors from Egypt—and the air was filled with the scent of roasted lamb and bitter herbs. But this meal would be different. For three years, the disciples had followed Jesus across dusty roads and stormy seas. They had seen miracles, heard parables, and felt the hope of a kingdom coming. Yet that night, as they reclined together, Jesus knew what they did not: before the next sunset, He would be betrayed, arrested, and led to the cross.

As the meal began, a quiet tension hung in the room. The disciples argued softly about who among them was greatest. Without a word, Jesus rose from the table, removed His outer garment, and wrapped a towel around His waist. Then He knelt—God Himself kneeling—and began to wash their feet one by one. The water splashed softly as He moved from person to person, wiping away the dust of their journey. Peter resisted at first, shocked that his Teacher would take a servant's role, but Jesus said, "Unless I wash you, you have no part with Me." In that act, He wasn't just cleaning their feet; He was showing them what love looks like when it stoops low.

When He finished, He returned to His place and said, "Now that I, your Lord and Teacher, have washed your feet, you also should wash one another's." Then, breaking bread, He gave thanks and handed it to them. "This is My body, given for you. Do this in remembrance of Me." He lifted the cup and said, "This is My blood, poured out for many for the forgiveness of sins." It was the first communion—the moment love took shape in bread and wine.

Later that night, they walked to the Garden of Gethsemane, where olive trees whispered in the wind. There, under the weight of what was coming, Jesus knelt again—this time in agony. "Father, if You are willing, take this cup from Me; yet not My will, but Yours be done." His sweat fell like drops of blood as He prayed, and His disciples, unable to comprehend the depth of His sorrow, fell asleep nearby. Even in His loneliness, Jesus chose surrender.

When soldiers arrived to arrest Him, He did not run. The One who had washed feet now offered His wrists to chains. His mission was not to fight, but to serve—to love until the very end.

That night around the table and in the garden, Jesus redefined greatness. It wasn't about power or position, but humility, sacrifice, and love that kneels before others.

WHAT IT MEANS

The Last Supper and Gethsemane show that real strength is found in serving and surrendering. Jesus' love wasn't only spoken—it was demonstrated, even when it cost everything.

 ## LIFE LESSON

True leadership begins with humility. When you choose to serve rather than be served, you reflect the heart of Jesus.

 ## TRY THIS

Do one quiet act of service this week—something small and unnoticed, like helping someone who won't thank you. Let it be your reminder that love often whispers louder than words.

 ## DID YOU KNOW?

The word Gethsemane means "oil press." It's fitting, as Jesus prayed there under immense spiritual pressure before His crucifixion. Olive trees from that ancient grove still grow on the Mount of Olives today.

 ## WORDS TO KNOW

Sacrifice – giving up something valuable for the sake of love or purpose.

 ## SHORT PRAYER

God, teach me to love like Jesus did—to serve without seeking recognition and to obey even when it's hard. Help me remember that humility is the highest form of strength and that love is never wasted. Amen.

49 Love Wins — Cross & Resurrection (Luke 23-24; John 20)

The sky darkened long before evening fell. Outside the city walls of Jerusalem, the crowd that had once shouted "Hosanna" now cried, "Crucify Him!" Soldiers led Jesus to a hill called Golgotha, the Place of the Skull. His body bore the marks of their cruelty, His hands and feet nailed to a wooden cross. Around Him stood soldiers, mockers, and a few heartbroken friends. Yet even in agony, His words were filled with mercy: "Father, forgive them, for they know not what they do."

As the hours passed, the earth seemed to mourn. The sun hid its face, and the ground trembled.

Hanging between heaven and earth, Jesus bore the weight of every sin, every sorrow, every failure humanity would ever know. When He finally breathed His last, He whispered, "It is finished." At that moment, the temple curtain tore in two, symbolizing that the barrier between God and humanity had been forever removed. Love had done what law and sacrifice never could—it had made a way back home.

Joseph of Arimathea and Nicodemus, quiet followers of Jesus, carefully took His body down and placed it in a new tomb carved into rock. A heavy stone was rolled across the entrance, and silence settled over the city. The disciples hid, crushed by grief, their hope sealed behind that stone.

But dawn has a way of rewriting endings. On the third day, as the sun rose, women who loved Him came to the tomb with spices for His body. When they arrived, the stone was gone. The tomb was empty. Angels appeared and said, "Why do you look for the living among the dead? He is not here; He has risen!" Their hearts raced with awe and fear. They ran to tell the others, breathless with the news that would change the world.

That same evening, Jesus appeared to His disciples. The doors were locked, fear thick in the room—but suddenly, there He was, standing among them. "Peace be with you," He said. The scars were still in His hands, yet death had no claim on Him anymore. He had conquered the grave, not through force, but through love. The cross that seemed like defeat had become victory.

From that day forward, every shadow carried the hint of light, every failure the possibility of redemption. Love had faced death and won. And the empty tomb still whispers the same truth to every heart that feels lost: no sin is too great, no night too dark, no ending too final for the power of God's love.

WHAT IT MEANS

The resurrection shows that love is stronger than sin, darkness, and even death itself. Jesus' victory is not just His—it's ours too. Hope lives because He lives.

 LIFE LESSON

When life feels broken beyond repair, remember that the story isn't over. God can turn even the darkest moment into resurrection.

 TRY THIS

Think of one area in your life that feels hopeless. Write down the words "It is finished," then cross them out and write, "He is risen." Let that remind you that God always has the final word.

 DID YOU KNOW?

Roman crucifixion was designed to humiliate and terrify. Yet through it, Jesus fulfilled ancient prophecies and transformed the cross—a symbol of death—into one of everlasting hope.

 WORDS TO KNOW

Redemption – being rescued or restored through the sacrifice of another.

 SHORT PRAYER

God, thank You for defeating death and proving that love never fails. When I face despair, remind me of the empty tomb. Help me live each day with the courage and joy of resurrection hope. Amen.

50 Power to Begin — Pentecost & the Early Church (Acts 2; 4:32-35)

Jerusalem hummed with celebration. It was the Feast of Pentecost, when Jews from every nation gathered to honor God's provision. The city was alive with voices, prayers, and songs. In a small upper room nearby, the followers of Jesus waited together—just as He had told them to do. Since His resurrection, they had seen the impossible. They had touched His scars, heard His promise, and watched Him ascend into heaven. Yet now, they waited—unsure what would come next, but trusting that it would come from God.

Suddenly, the stillness broke. A sound like a roaring wind filled the house, shaking the walls and hearts alike.

Flames appeared—not burning with destruction, but glowing with divine fire—and rested above each believer's head. They were filled with the Holy Spirit, the very presence of God now living inside them. As they began to speak, their words came out in languages they'd never learned, reaching the ears of the international crowd outside. People stopped and stared. "How is it that we hear them in our own tongue?" they asked. Confusion turned to wonder.

Then Peter, the same man who had once denied Jesus out of fear, stood up with new boldness. His voice carried over the noise: "This is what was spoken by the prophet Joel. God has poured out His Spirit on all people!" He told them about Jesus—His life, death, and resurrection—and about the forgiveness available through Him. The message cut straight to their hearts. That day, three thousand people believed, were baptized, and joined the growing movement that would become the church.

But the miracle didn't stop there. The believers began living as one family. They met daily, praying, eating together, and sharing everything they had. No one was left hungry, lonely, or forgotten. Those with extra sold their possessions so that everyone's needs could be met. The same Spirit that had filled them with words now filled them with love, generosity, and courage. Through their unity, others saw something different—something real.

The early church wasn't built on power, wealth, or buildings. It was built on hearts ignited by the Spirit of God. Each act of kindness, each prayer, each shared meal became a spark spreading across the world. From that upper room to distant nations, the fire kept burning. The promise Jesus made—that His followers would be His witnesses "to the ends of the earth"—had begun to unfold.

The story of Pentecost isn't just about wind and flame—it's about transformation. Ordinary people became carriers of extraordinary power, and through them, the world began to change.

What It Means

Pentecost marks the moment when God's Spirit came to dwell within His people, giving them strength to live with purpose. The same power that filled the first believers still works through anyone who says yes to God today.

 ### Life Lesson

You're never too ordinary for God to use. His Spirit turns hesitation into boldness and community into unstoppable love.

 ### Try This

Take five minutes today to thank God for the gifts He's already given you—kindness, creativity, courage. Ask Him to show you one way to use those gifts this week to encourage or help someone else.

 ### Did You Know?

The word Pentecost comes from the Greek for "fiftieth," marking fifty days after Passover. It was originally a harvest festival, making it the perfect backdrop for the spiritual "harvest" of new believers that day.

 ### Words to Know

Empowerment – receiving strength or ability from God to do what you couldn't do alone.

 ### Short Prayer

God, thank You for sending Your Spirit to live within us. Fill me with the same courage, compassion, and unity that shaped the first believers. Help me use my life to spread Your love wherever I go. Amen.

www.ingramcontent.com/pod-product-compliance
Lightning Source LLC
Chambersburg PA
CBHW060046230426
43661CB00004B/681